The Complete Idiot's Reference Card

Sarah's Ten Favorite Things to Do With Your Dog

1. **Wag Your Tail.** Some tricks just come naturally. Say this phrase in a happy voice and watch that tail go! Other everyday behaviors also can be put on commands, such as Kiss and Bow.

2. **High Five.** Once your dog learns Paw you can expand his repertoire to other commands such as High Five, Low Five, and Paws Up. Once your dog knows these cool greeting techniques, he'll climb up five rungs on the social scale.

3. **Hooping It Up.** All dogs jump—they just need a little education on what to jump on or through. Teaching your dog jumping tricks, such as jumping through a hoop, can wow your audience as well as give him the opportunity to vent his excitement.

4. **Speak.** Some dogs just can't say enough! To harness your dog's vocal chords, teach him to speak on command. Once he learns what he's barking for, you can teach him the magical off command, Quiet.

5. **Fetch the Paper.** What better way to start your day? All you need is a dog that loves to carry things. Take your dog out each morning, say Fetch the Paper and praise him for carrying it in to you. Don't forget a tasty treat for a job well done.

6. **Sniff and Find.** Detective dog to the rescue! Show your dog a treat, command Sniff, tell him Stay while you hide it, then release him with Okay, Find. Soon you'll be able to hide the treats in the next room and watch your dog sniff them out.

7. **Disco Dancer.** If your dog's happier on two paws than four, you'll need to add this trick to his repertoire. At arm's length, hold your dog's favorite treat above his nose and say Dance. Is there any partner more appealing? (This trick has special appeal for the toy breed who just can't stand being overlooked!)

8. **Frisbee Finesse.** If you have an active dog who never runs out of gas and you can't seem to toss a tennis ball far enough, perhaps it's time to consider exchanging the ball for a flying disc. More exhilarating and challenging for your dog, the Frisbee will keep him on his paws wondering where you'll toss it next.

9. **Awesome Agility.** Agility is catching on everywhere. Similar to equestrian jumping events but way more fun, this sport tests a dog's ability to balance coordination and speed, and the handler's ability to keep the dog focused and directed.

10. **Pet Therapy.** A good doggy deed, pet therapy allows you to share the joy your dog gives to you. If your dog can't seem to get enough attention and love and seems to want nothing more than a warm lap to rest on, this could be the activity for you.

alpha
books

Active and Healthy Is as Easy as One, Two, Three!

1. **A Clean Bill of Health.** Before beginning any of the activities in this book, visit the veterinarian and make sure your dog is in good health.

2. **Routine Care.** You're responsible for the everyday care and maintenance of your dog's health. Clear out a drawer and stock it with brushes, nail clippers, cotton swabs, tooth cleaning supplies, and any medications or vitamins. A first aid kit also is a must.

3. **Water.** Dogs dehydrate very quickly. Make sure fresh water is always available wherever you go.

Sarah Says Click a Trick!

Clicker fever is sweeping the nation. A small, hand-held box, this device helps you point out to your dog the exact behavior you're trying to get her to do. A click, followed by a food reward, will excite your dog and give both of you a whole new outlook on training.

Know Your Dog's Personality

Any dog can learn tricks, but dogs do best at tasks that match their personality. Which canine profile most closely matches your own best friend?

Eager Beavers. These guys will do whatever it takes to make you happy. If you toss a ball, they'll bring it back 500 times; if you encourage them to jump, they'll jump on you and everyone else. With this dog, all you have to do is think of a trick, sport, or activity.

Joe Cools. Laid back and relaxed, these guys are in control of every situation and are less focused on you than on their own image. They need help in the motivation department; check out the clicker training and other motivational devices to encourage your cool dude.

Comedians. Quick-minded perfectionists, Comedians are revved up wonder dogs who get into a lot of trouble if they're not directed. Trick training and sports activities are a good positive outlet for all their undirected energy.

Bullies. These dogs take themselves far too seriously. Clicker training is a must, as it will give this dog something to work for. Directing their breed instincts into a sports activity is also a great idea.

Sweetie Pies. Docile and mild, these dogs like to observe situations rather than control them. Trick training will raise their confidence level and encourage them to interact with you rather than to observe from the sidelines.

Nervous Nells. These dogs view the world from behind your legs. Trick training and activities are essential to make them feel more secure. Gentle training and use of the clicker will give them a much more positive outlook.

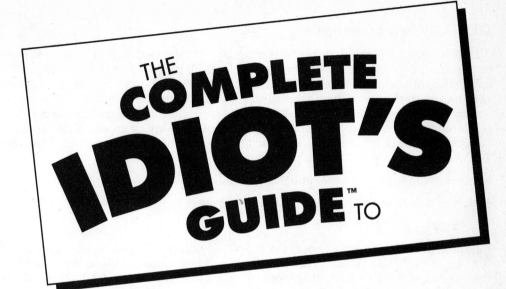

THE COMPLETE IDIOT'S GUIDE™ TO

Fun and Tricks With Your Dog

by Sarah Hodgson

alpha
books

A Division of Macmillan General Reference
A Simon & Schuster Macmillan Company
1633 Broadway New York, NY 10019-6705

International Standard Book Number: 0-87605-083-6

Library of Congress Catalog Card Number: 97-2544

99 98 97   4 3 2 1

Interpretation of the printing code: the rightmost number of the first series of numbers is the year of the book's printing; the rightmost number of the second series of numbers is the number of the book's printing. For example, a printing code of 97-1 shows that the first printing occurred in 1997.

Printed in the United States of America

Managing Editor
Brian Phair

Editor
Beth Adelman

Production Editor
Linda Seifert

Illustrator
Judd Winick

Designer
Glenn Larsen

Cover Designer
Michael Freeland

Line Artists
Casey Price
Laura Robbins
Marvin Van Tiem

Indexer
Robert Long

Production Team
Angela Calvert
Maureen West

Contents at a Glance

Contents

Introduction

Why a fun and tricks book dedicated to idiots? Well, don't take the idiot part personally—I didn't pick the title. But there's been such hoopla over the original *The Complete Idiot's Guide to Choosing, Raising, and Training a Dog* (I wrote that one, too!) that the publishers thought it natural I should follow up with a more light-hearted, fun-loving version.

Aside from writing the first *Idiot's Guide* for dogs, I'm a dog maniac who for years has been trying to take the edge off of serious training and inject the whole process with a little fun. After all, isn't one of the primary reasons we share our lives with dogs to enjoy their company while they help us loosen our grip on this no-nonsense, career-driven world?

Don't get me wrong! I'm not negating the whole training process. After all, I am a dog trainer and basic lessons are essential to let your dog know who's in charge. But once you've made that point, you can lighten up. (And if you haven't made that point yet, you have been trained by your dog. Chapter 1 is dedicated to you. You need to be the trainer, not the trained, before you can move on to tricks and games.)

Though I'm something of a stickler in my obedience techniques, games and tricks have few rules. Lessons should be short, quick, and fun. And, unlike formal training where I limit the treats and toy rewards to keep your dog's focus on you, I encourage food lures, rewards, and praise when teaching tricks and fun.

Are there any limitations to joining in the fun described herein? No! Tricks and games are open to dogs of all sizes, shapes, and ages. Of course, there are two hundred and some-odd pages here dedicated to games and tricks, and it's likely not every page will be for you and your dog. You'd have to be a magician to transform a pack of Pekingese into a dog sled team. But that many pages leaves plenty of room for a whole array of games and tricks for the everyday dog and owner, and some extra space for more complex maneuvers and team hobbies such as Agility and pet therapy. Every dog can learn to do *something*.

So let the fun begin! Like my other *Idiot's Guide*, you can read this book cover to cover, or surf the table of contents and create your own starting point. I've arranged the chapters in order of complexity: simple stuff first, then fancy, with movie star-potential tricks a little further down the road.

What I Do All Day

Writing is not my day job. In real life I'm a dog trainer. I've been in the business of helping dogs and people for nearly twelve years, and I've often said that no one has it better; I'm earning a living at what I love to do. I feel pretty blessed!

Activities in my day vary between writing, private classes, group lessons, puppy classes, aggression rehab—it's never quite the same. There is a common theme, however, that runs throughout everything I do. I insist that my clients lighten up and teach their dogs something they'll enjoy. A Poodle, for example, must learn to dance. A retriever needs to fetch. Bichon Frises love their parlor tricks. Huskies want to pull a sled, herders love to herd, and so on.

Though I don't have a résumé with names like Lassie, Benji, and more modern television stars like Eddie from *Frasier* and Murray from *Mad About You*, I do have a history of igniting the imagination and motivation of dog owners to discover the magic and fun that twinkles in their dog's eyes, and to make the most of it.

Sharing your life with a dog shouldn't be a militaristic venture, selfishly designed around what you want your dog to do. Owning a dog is about joining two different species, two different spirits, in a way that will make the world better for both.

Decoding the Text

Since this is an *Idiot's Guide,* I will assume you know nothing. Please don't think I'm patronizing you if I explain a term you've known for years, but I don't want to leave anyone out in the cold. Teaching dogs brings us together as a family, so be supportive.

One of the cool extras in reading (and writing) this book are the sidebar boxes that are sprinkled throughout the text. They're added to draw your attention to important information, or just facts that are fun to know.

Bet You Didn't Know

These boxes offer insights, secrets, little extras I've picked up over the course of my career—stuff I wouldn't want you to miss.

Grrr

Don't forget to read the Grrr warning boxes! These will caution you about common errors, dangerous habits, and things you should avoid.

Hand Signals

These boxes explain the silent signals you can teach your dog, so you can put him through his paces without saying a word.

Sarah Says

These Sarah Says tips simplify each process and clue you in to shortcuts or points you really must remember. They may also highlight how to handle dogs with special characteristics.

Acknowledgments

As usual, I'm wowed by the many people it takes to complete a project. My first thank you goes to Sean Frawley, my publisher, who year after year and book after book has been a rock of support and a dear friend. Next, a warm thank you to my primary editor, Beth Adelman, who had tough shoes to fill and did a great job. Thank you, thank you for all your help. My appreciation also goes out to all those behind the scenes—illustrators, editors, and production people at Alpha—who are the unsung heroes of every project.

A bottomless thank you to my support team, without whose help and advice I would never have the peace of mind to get out of bed each morning: Judi Kestenbaum, Laurie Guarino, Lucille D'Urso, Katherine Votkins, Faith Krasnow, and Farah and Russ Mehta. You are the best of the best!

And finally, a huge thank you to my trick crew, without whose good humor and patient practice this book would not have been possible: Ali, Shari, and Bob; Alice and June; Anna, Carolyn, and John; Buddy, Laurie, and Wendy; Chase and Farah; Darby, Jill, and Alan; Lily and Katherine; Morgan, Judy, Jeff, and family; Mr. Mann and Marion; Penny and Grace; Taz and Claudia. Happy tails to all!

Just one more. A very special thank you to my photographer, John Geoff. You were a true Godsend.

Consider your face licked all over!

Trademarks

All terms mentioned in this book that are known to be or are suspected of being trademarks or service marks have been appropriately capitalized. Alpha Books and Macmillan General Reference cannot attest to the accuracy of this information. Use of a term in this book should not be regarded as affecting the validity of any trademark or service mark.

Part 1
Putting the Best Paw Forward

Whether you're starting with a young dog or an old one, big or small, teaching fun and useful tricks is a real blast. Before you teach your dog any new routine, however, from fetching the paper to limping soulfully across a movie set, you'll need to look at things from his perspective. Dogs can't read your mind. Each new request must be broken down into bite-sized pieces and laid out in a format that is fun to learn. If your dog looks confused and you get frustrated or angry, the lesson's over. Trick training requires incredible patience. Don't worry though—even Lassie wasn't trained in a day.

In this first section you'll discover what motivates your dog, and how his personality will guide you through the teaching process. In addition, you'll get a crash course on dog psychology and basic training, so you're consistent with your words and techniques as you surf through the rest of the book.

Chapter 1

Calling All Dogs

In This Chapter

➤ Evolution and dog breeds

➤ Personality profiles

➤ A puppy head start program

Take a look at your dog. What have you got? Big or small? Active or a couch potato? Puppy or adult? Before you introduce your dog to this book, get a handle on who he is: Where he's from, his personality and age. Dogs are like snowflakes, thumbprints and children—they're all unique. Each one will respond to training differently.

For example, a fetching enthusiast will return a ball until your arm falls off, whereas a non-retriever will look at you cross-eyed and leave the ball where you threw it. Knowing your dog's breed characteristics and personality profile is a must before you get started. Not sure what I'm talking about? Read on; this chapter will teach you.

Sarah Says
    In the United States, there are 140 breeds recognized by the American Kennel Club. The AKC is in charge of assigning a number to and counting every single pure-bred puppy born in America. What a job! When I try to make sense of it, I think it is a lot like a school: You have seven different classes and one principal's office, the AKC, that keeps everything organized.

Breed Specifics

Open any dog book and you'll see lots of different dogs. Big dogs. Small dogs. All-sizes-in-between dogs. Dogs with short hair. Dogs with long hair. Dogs with *no hair*! What's going on here? All these different dogs belong to different *breeds*. A breed is a group of dogs that are all the same size, have the same hair style and act pretty much the same.

In America, breeds are categorized into seven groups: Sporting, Hound, Working, Terrier, Non-Sporting, Toy and Herding. These groups are organized by the American Kennel Club, or AKC, according to shared characteristics. One thing's for sure—different breeds do different things.

To know what tricks and activities you and your dog will get the most of, take a look at his breed.

The Sporting Group

Originally bred to spend entire days running in the fields seeking out and collecting land and water fowl for their masters, this bunch is still pretty hung up on the retrieving thing. They're an energetic, loyal, happy lot who thrive on interaction. Trusting, friendly and eager to please, they take to training (both trick and obedience) well and generally view each new exercise as an adventure.

Labrador Retriever

An over-disciplined or untrained sporting dog, on the other hand, will use all his coopera-tive, retrieving skills against you. Instead of bringing you objects, he'll play keep-away. Call him and he'll stay just out of reach. Ignore him and he'll bark at you. Trained or untrained, helpful or bothersome, endearing or annoying—it's up to you.

The Hound Group

These guys were bred to course fast-moving game, with hunters in quick pursuit. Dogs with a mission! Active, lively and rugged, they have been domesticated into fun-loving, gentle pets who have a high spirit for adventure.

Greyhound

Not bred to look to humans for direction, they usually don't. Consequently, obedience training can be slow and challenging; hounds would rather trail a rabbit than hang out doing Sit-Stays. Trick training, however, with its use of food and toy lures, takes on a whole new meaning. Hounds excel in activities that require their nose, and if you put them in the spotlight these guys are real hams.

Grrr
A leash or enclosure is required when hounds are outside. Although stubborn when it comes to training, they're still a lot of fun.

The Working Group

This is the most diversified group in terms of their breed functions. Some pull sleds, others guard flocks, and others protect the homestead. They do however, have one common thread: They've all worked in the past to serve people.

Siberian Husky

A dog with a history like that can't be ignored! Obedience training is a must, though after those skills are mastered, trick and activity training is a natural adjunct. Not quick to embarrass themselves doing circus routines, however, they prefer more complex, multi-step tasks that put their minds to work.

Though more patience may be required with certain routines, these guys can learn anything. On the other hand, an untrained working dog is lost. Unemployment leaves them bored, nervous and, in some cases, territorial and aggressive.

The Herding Group

These dogs were bred to move flocks and herds. Agile and alert, they're quick to figure out if the people they live with are smart enough to be considered shepherds or passive sheep. If you're a sheep your herder will run circles around you. If you're his shepherd, training will come quickly and easily.

Ready to master anything new, they make great trick dogs and excel in agility games. Isolated or ignored, they may develop timidity, barking, or pacing habits.

Collie

The Terrier Group

Originally bred to control the rodent population in many European countries (especially on the British Isles), these dogs are a self-assured, spirited, and lively bunch. Agile and independent, they don't excel in off-leash obedience training and need to be leashed outdoors.

Trick training, however, is a different story. Terriers love the spotlight. As happy on two legs as they are on four, they'll dazzle you with their athletic feats. Great candidates for this trick and activity book, they'll leave you in a fit of hysterics marveling at their spunk, quick mindedness, and good humor. Untrained or over isolated, however, these little acrobats can become chronic barkers, destructive chewers, and urine markers, or may develop aggression over objects, food, and with other animals.

West Highland White Terrier

The Non-Sporting Group

Unlike other groups, there is little consistency in personalities here because the non-sporting dogs were all bred for different tasks. One thing *is* consistent though—they're all lovable! Some take to trick training better than others. A Dalmatian, for example, will slide into a tutu much more readily than a Lhasa Apso.

Many of these breeds were originally bred for specific work, but because work is hard to come by these days, they've become companions. If you've got a dog from this category, consult breed-specific books to figure out what yours likes to do.

Miniature Poodle

The Toy Group

These dogs were bred 'for one thing and one thing only—to be companions. In keeping with their ancestors, they continue to perfect the art of being adorable. Playful and affectionate, toys love the spotlight, and if the end result of a trick session is more attention, they'll be happy to cooperate. Don't get your little handful confused with a working breed, however. If the task is too difficult or you're not praising them enough, they just might go on strike.

Grrr

It's easy to neglect any type of training with toy dogs, but owner beware! Without direction they can become quite tyrannical, ruling the house with constant barking and snapping. To get the most from these little guys, train them to do some useful tricks, endearing them to one and all.

Anyone who has ever shared their life with a small dog will tell you they're adorable, especially when they're puppies. Spoiling them almost seems to go with the territory. After all, their behavior is so miniaturized that's rarely a problem. However, living the unstructured life, being doted on night and day is just as harmful for their psyche. The result? What I call *Small Dog Syndrome*. Sound familiar? If obedience is too structured for you, try trick training. Little dogs take to it like a fish to water, and seeing them perform is a real hoot.

Shih Tzu

A Word About Mixed Breeds

If you have a mixed breed dog, don't despair! Your job is a twice the fun. First, see if you can identify the mix. If you're not sure, get a professional opinion. After you've got a rough sketch, read over each dog group. Then, on to the fun part—the observational experiment. It's time to study your dog's behavior and decide where he fits in. I know a Shepherd-Retriever mix, Charley, who's the spitting image of Rin-Tin-Tin but who'd retrieve a ball for you until the cows came home.

A friendly mixed breed dog. This one looks like part shepherd and part polar breed, but who knows?

Bet You Didn't Know

There is a theory afloat known as Hybrid Vigor. It contends that due to their larger and more diverse gene pools, mixed breed dogs are superior in health and temperament to pure-bred dogs. What do I think? The theory sounds good to me. There are a lot of inherited health problems in certain breeds, such as hip dysplasia. Regarding temperament, I've loved just as many pure as mixed. The choice is up to you.

Personality Profiles

After you understand your dog's ancestry, you'll need to take an individual look at his personality. Like us, they're all different, and how they relate to the world directly affects how they'll relate to you, their teacher.

I have identified six character types of dogs that I'll refer to throughout the rest of the book. Read them over and identify yours.

Eager Beaver

As trick dogs, these creatures will do whatever it takes to make you happy, although they can be difficult and manic if ignored. Presented with new material, it's almost as if they're racing the clock to figure out what you want.

You'll notice they excel in tricks that approximate what their particular breed was designed to do. With this dog, all you have to do is decide what's next and it's done. Though enthusiasm and staying power are a must, harsh techniques will crush their spirit.

Joe Cool

These fellows are laid back and relaxed, and not terribly interested in organized activities. Obedience puts them to sleep, and when it comes to tricks you might get a teenage eye roll when you request "Paw."

Every dog has his weak spot however—perhaps cheese or dried liver—and after you discover it, you'll be amazed at how quickly your mellow fellow will come to life. Lessons must be kept short and your enthusiasm high to keep these guys awake and interested.

Here's Morgan with his sunglasses on, being extremely cool.

Comedian

These guys are the Danny Kaye of the dog world. They live for a laugh. Wonder dogs, they'll figure out a routine before you've had a chance to learn it yourself.

Quick-minded perfectionists, comedians will get into a lot of trouble if they're not directed.

Bully

These dogs take themselves far too seriously. In a group of dogs they would be destined to lead, and your home is no different. Unless you're an experienced trainer, dogs with this nature can be difficult to train for anything.

Obedience training is a must, and although they're often turned off by frivolous tricks, they excel in organized activities such as tracking or agility.

Sweetie Pie

Docile and mild, these dogs like to observe situations rather than control them. Where obedience training makes them feel more secure about situations, tricks and organized

Sarah Says
Once I was caught in a traffic jam with a dog who fancied himself a comedian, and before the cars started to roll he had learned to deliver the car phone to me when it rang!

Grrr
If your dog is a bully and he threatens you, call a professional trainer *now*!

activities help build their confidence. They adore the people they love and train best under a soft, patient hand. Yelling or hitting frightens them terribly, even when it's not directed at them.

Nervous Nell

These dogs like to view their world from behind your legs. Be patient and forgiving when teaching new maneuvers, and you'll notice how eager your dog is to please you. Training is essential to help these dogs feel more secure and to build their confidence.

Sarah Says
All puppies love treat cups. To make your own, get a few disposable plastic cups and some treats or Cheerios breakfast cereal. Fill each cup one-third full with treats or cereal, and spread them around the house. Each time you pass one, shake it and call out your puppy's name. Soon he'll pay attention every time you call him, treat cup or not.

Puppy Head Start

Although you can definitely teach your old dog new tricks, don't start your puppy too young. It takes twelve weeks for their brains to completely develop, and another month or two for their attention span to mature. Wait until your puppy is at least four months old before you introduce him to the routines in this book. Learning anything, even fun tricks, is stressful.

But don't put this book back on the shelf just yet. If you've got a young puppy chewing on your shoelace, you can get a head start on his movie star potential by observing and interacting with his everyday play. Listed in this section are some characteristics that will help you identify your pup's natural abilities.

Retrieving Rover

This fellow likes to put everything in his mouth. Toys, shoes, paper towels—it's all the same in his eyes. Correcting a young puppy is like yelling at an infant; it doesn't register. Instead, encourage your pup to show you his "prize" by praising him every time he picks something up, and reward every delivery with a treat from the treat cup. You may think you're rewarding delinquent chewing, but in fact, chewing itself will not become a problem because your pup will be happy to show you his treasure. Think of it this way: Yelling at a puppy when he grabs a sock is perceived as prize envy (you want what he has), and that's what results in destructive chewing.

Sarah Says
When your puppy brings back one of his own toys, give him extra treats and take some time out for play.

Circus Clown

These peppy, bright creatures are as happy on two paws as they are on four. Alert and inquisitive, they want to be in on everything and are drawn to laughter. Needless to say, their forwardness can be quite annoying if you don't redirect their energy. Fortunately they love to learn and you can start learning a lot of natural routines from the start.

When they are hopping around on two legs, tell them, "Dance." If they put their paws on you, look to the ceiling and ignore them. Soon they'll catch on to the game and dance on their own.

Elbows on the floor, tail in the air, the play bow is a favorite ready position for the clown. If you see one, press your hands against your knees in delight and say, "Take a Bow." Monkey see, monkey do!

These guys get very impatient when the attention is off them. To regain the spotlight they have many routines, one of which is barking at you. When this happens, turn to your dog and say, "Speak-Speak." After ten seconds say "Quiet" and ignore them.

A+ Academic

These guys are the engineers of the dog world. Observant and keenly aware, these pups do as well in multistep tasks and tricks as adult dogs. For now, play hide-and-seek games to keep their minds sharp.

Holding your pup's collar, show him a treat and say, "Sniff." If he reaches out to snatch it, pull him back. Toss the treat five inches in front of you and make him wait. When he's calm say, "Go Find" and let go of the collar. Progressively toss the treat further, then have someone hide it around a corner or under the edge of a rug. As your pup gets better, you can hide two or three treats in more challenging places.

Practice the race-around recall with two or more people. Have everyone to stand about ten feet apart, each with a treat cup. Call your puppy back and forth using his name and lots of encouragement. After he catches on, have one person hide around a corner or behind a tree while your puppy is racing around. Increase the difficulty of your hiding spots as he catches on.

Agile Athlete

The Huckleberry Finn of the dog world, these guys end up in the darndest places, and correcting them only increases their mischief. Setting up an obstacle course in your house or backyard can tone down

Grrr
Make your jumps are at least one inch lower than your puppy's shoulder blades. Jumping too high can permanently damage growing muscles and joints.

13

their curious streak. Be creative—brooms or logs to hurdle, a tunnel to zip through, or an old tire to climb on. If your house and yard are too small, use what you can find at a local park.

Dog-Gone Digger

Is your puppy into everything? Are your house plants being uprooted? You need a game to redirect your pup's impulses. As often as possible (once a week is fine if you live in a city) put on garden gloves, stuff some biscuits in your pocket, and take your puppy to a good digging area. Say, "Go dig" and start digging yourself, like a dog, burying his treats as you go. Soon it will be a mud slinging free-for-all, and your house plants will be forever in your debt.

Discovering your pup's natural talents can be a real adventure!

The Least You Need to Know

➤ Certain breeds will have character traits that naturally lend themselves to specific tricks and activities. Know the instincts and limitations of your dog's breed before you get started.

➤ Dogs, like people, have distinct personalities, and some are definitely more into learning than others. Fortunately, every dog has a weak spot. Whether it's cheese or liver or a toy, it's your job to find something your dog can't live without.

➤ You *can* teach your old dog new tricks, but you shouldn't start structured training with a puppy under four months old. If you've got an eight-week-old nibbler, participate in play sessions and keep on the look-out for his natural abilities.

Performance Prerequisites

Before you teach that dog of yours dog how to serve you breakfast in bed, you must make sure you can get his attention. Otherwise he'll be the one teaching you tricks... ever see the owner-chasing-the-dog routine? It's hysterical, but very unsafe. Don't be scared; we're not going for show ring Obedience. Just the basics, boiled down to seven foundation commands I call *the Magic Seven*.

To be a fair and fun teacher you'll also need to master Doglish, your dog's native language. Until you learn to think *with* and not *against* your dog, you can't teach him properly. It's impossible for your dog to be human, no matter how much you work together. So how do you talk dog? It's quite an adventure.

Doglish

We speak English. Our dogs speak Doglish. To be a good teacher, you must put yourself in their paws. Words don't carry the same weight; lengthy explanations leave them puzzled. Doglish consists of three simple elements: eye contact, body language, and tone.

Eye Contact

My Aunt Polly always says you can read the attraction two people have for one another by watching their eyes. Dogs aren't much different. If yours looks to you with eyes that are trusting and eager, you'll have no trouble teaching your dog anything. If you can't get a blink, you'll have to do some preliminary "respect" work, as outlined later in this chapter in the section called "The Magic Seven."

Stand up straight and make eye contact with your dog. It's about respect.

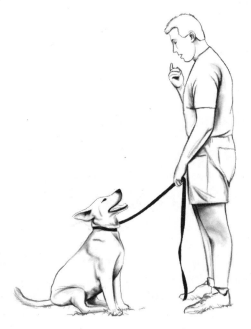

Body Language

Body language is a funny thing. As a species, we humans often overlook its power to communicate. Picture this: You're trying to teach your dog to jump through a hoop. Every time he gets to the hoop, however, he runs around it. Poor thing—he's a little nervous. You try again, but he dodges. You squeeze through yourself several times, saying, "See? Like this." Now he thinks you've lost your mind. You get frustrated. Your body tenses, eyes bulge, hands clench. Now he has a reason to avoid the hoop.

Training calls for a relaxed and patient body posture. I call it the *peacock position*: Stand upright and proud.

Tone

Tone is a huge part of the training process. If you yell at your dog, you'll either freak him out or look like a fool, depending on his personality profile. If you speak sweetly, you'll encourage playfulness.

To encourage your dog's attention there is only one tone to use: the directive tone. It's clear, direct and non-threatening. Don't worry though, it's easy to master. Just use your regular voice with an ounce of over-enunciation. Think of your dog as a two-year-old learning their first two-syllable word. After your dog learns a particular behavior, you'll be able to whisper commands. But in the beginning, speak clearly.

Attitude

Attitude is everything. If your dog thinks you're cool, you can teach him anything he's physically capable of learning. By nature, dogs relate to a hierarchical system where one leader rules over all.

What determines who's boss? Not Rambo-like fighting power, but mental stamina. Leaders keep their heads while others all about them are un-nerved. When there is confusion, all look to the head honcho for stability. The leader directs, structures, and reassures. For any type of training to be effective, you need to assume the roll of leader. Let's start.

Sarah Says
Imagine a peacock, beautiful and proud, chest out, confident and in control. When giving your dog a direction or command, throw your shoulders back and stand tall like a peacock. Tell your friends and family about this peacock position and start strutting your stuff!

Hand Signals
You can start teaching your dog hand signals as soon as he masters each trick. It's pretty nifty and also encourages better eye contact. I'll suggest one for each new routine. Eventually you'll be able to direct your dog with a slight flick of the wrist. Abracadabra!

Sarah Says
Got a multiperson household? A whole brood perhaps? You'll need to help everyone establish a hierarchy that starts with two-legged critters and ends with four-legged ones.

Outfitting Your Dog

If your dog hasn't had any training, or he needs some brushing up, you'll need a quick refresher course before you move on. For one thing, your dog will need to be well mannered on a leash and responsive to basic commands. Fortunately, you don't need to be a brain surgeon to master this stuff. Before we start, though, you need to outfit your dog with the right collar and leash.

Training Collars

The buckle collar is not to be confused with a training collar. The training collar is used exclusively when your dog is on a leash. The only dogs exempt are toy breeds and puppies under sixteen weeks of age, because their neck muscles are too weak for a training collar.

Sarah Says
Every dog must wear a buckle collar with identification tags at all times. Whether your dog is two months old or two years, two pounds or two hundred, find her a nice collar and attach those tags.

There are three types of training collars; choosing the one you use will depend on one thing—your dog. Because I can't be there to help you decide, you'll have to ask a knowledgeable person if you're confused. Trainers, veterinarians, or groomers may be helpful. Some dog people, however, are one-collar oriented and will tell you only one type will work. Shy away from that advice, because every situation, and every dog, is different. What may work wonders for you might be someone else's nightmare. Find a collar that works from the selection that follows (trying them all out if you have to), and go with it.

Some training collar options.

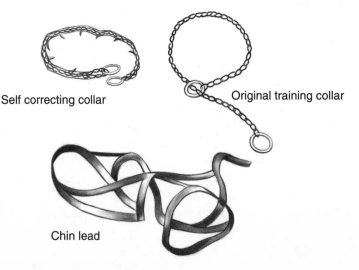

Self correcting collar

Original training collar

Chin lead

The Original Training Collar

I call this the original because it has been around the longest. It has some other names too, like a chain or choke collar, though if used properly it should never choke your dog. Choking and restraint only aggravate problems. Most people don't know that it is the sound of the collar, *not* the restraint, that teaches. A jingle of the chain is all it takes. I know everyone would rather use this collar properly than hear their dog hacking during walks, but most people don't know how to make the darn thing work.

To start with, make sure you put on the collar properly. If put on backward, this collar will cause your dear doggy lots of discomfort. Fitted improperly, the links will catch in a viselike hold around your dog's neck and do what the collar is not suppose to do—choke. Putting it on correctly, however, is a big challenge. It is one of the hardest lessons in my beginner class. Putting the collar on right is something people still mess up on graduation night!

Don't be discouraged if you get it wrong a time or two; just keep trying until you've got it right. First, decide which side you want your dog to walk on. You must be consistent, as dogs are easily confused. As left is traditional, I'll use left as my example:

➤ Take one loop of the collar and slide the slack part of the chain through it.

➤ Pretending you're on *Sesame Street*, make the letter P with the chain.

➤ Holding it out with the P facing you, stand *in front* of your dog. Show him your creation.

➤ With the P still facing you, slide the collar over the dog's head as you praise.

➤ To check the result, slide the rings up behind his ears and stand at his left side. Grasp the moveable ring and pull it toward your leg. Does it slide freely through the stationary loop (you got it!) or does it bend over the stationary loop (try again)?

If you still find yourself in a constant pulling battle with your dog, only broken by occasional hacking, you might want to investigate other collar options.

Grrr
Remember, it's the sound of the collar, not the restraint, that teaches! Used properly, a quick snap (which sounds like a zipper) will correct your dog's impulse to disobey or to lead.

Sarah Says
If your dog is fussy, give him a biscuit just before you slide the collar across his nose.

To put on a training collar, create the letter P with the chain and slide the collar over your dog's head.

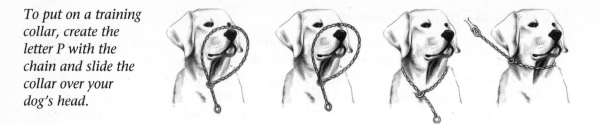

The Self Correcting Collar

Yes, I know it looks torturous. I can't argue its aesthetic qualities. But it is perfectly humane, I promise; especially if by using the original training collar you fall into the I-can't-stop-choking-my-dog category. The self correcting collar works on the quick external pinch-pain principle, which is far less damaging than a permanently crushed trachea.

Grrr

If you decide to try the self correcting collar, let me warn you of one thing: Very rarely these collars pop off. To prevent a possible emergency, buy an oversized nylon training collar and attach your leash to both when walking in an unconfined area.

This collar was developed by the Germans for many of their bull-necked breeds. I have found it works wonders for dogs who are pain-insensitive or too powerful to persuade with the plain-chain type collar. Although it's officially termed a prong collar, I refer to it as self correcting because it requires little strength to use. By simply locking your arm into place, even the rowdiest of dogs will feel a pinch and will slow down.

If you decide to give this collar a try, be sure to have an experienced authority help you fit your dog and give you a quick lesson on its use. You do not need to snap the leash with this collar; a simple pull usually does the trick.

The Chin Lead

Once again, I have renamed a product. What the heck, it's more descriptive. Actually, this product comes in two forms. The pet stores sell a version known as a *Halti*. The other brand is called a *Gentle Leader* and is sold exclusively through veterinarians.

I recommend this collar for clients struggling with an over-excitable or headstrong dog; a dog who is not persuaded by neck collars or who considers neck restraint to be confrontational. If you feel yourself in either of these traps, this may be the perfect solution. This collar eliminates the need to get into a choking battle and passively teaches your dog that you're in charge.

The chin lead works on the "mommy" principle. When your dog was a pup, his mom would correct him by grasping his muzzle and shaking it. This communicated, "Hey wild one, settle down!" The chin lead has the same effect. Left on during high energy times, it discourages rowdiness and mouthing, jumping and barking.

Leashes

There are two types of leashes. One is your six-foot garden-variety, made from either cotton, leather, or nylon. The second is a recent invention of mine that received two patents for design and methodology. I call it the *Teaching Lead* and it's useful in training basics and versatile for every day use. The difference between the two? One you hold and the other, the Teaching Lead, you wear.

Sound funky? Why would you want to wear a leash? I designed it to communicate leadership passively. Besides that, you can walk through town with your hands free. Pretty cool! (Have a look in the back of the book for information on where to buy the Teaching Lead.)

Sarah Says
Whatever leash you use, you must teach your dog that you're the one to watch.

When holding the leash, your hand is everything. Many people curl their fingers under the leash, which is incorrect. It encourages the dog to pull forward and lift up. Instead, hold the leash with your knuckles facing the sky and your thumb wrapped around the underside of the leash. Confused? Here's a little exercise: Hold your left arm straight out from your body. Pointing your thumb downward, lower your arm. As you do, curl your thumb under the lead and wrap your knuckles over the top.

The Magic Seven

Before you go any further, you need to make sure your dog understands the basics. He won't have to win ribbons in a show to move on to the fancy stuff, but he'll need to know seven key commands. I call them *the Magic Seven*:

➤ Name

➤ Name, Let's Go

➤ No Sir (or No Ma'am)

➤ Sit and Stay

➤ Wait and Okay (or Stand)

➤ Down

➤ Excuse Me

When I was a kid I remember taking a dog training class with an instructor who told everyone to practice twice a day for fifteen minutes. Not unusual or bad advice, but who can find the time in this fast-paced world we live in?

I'll tell you what I do now: I use the seven basic commands conversationally throughout the day. Sit before petting or treats, Excuse Me when a dog's under foot, Let's Go to change direction, and No for the naughty stuff. Without taking time out of your day, you can teach your dog the Magic Seven too.

Bet You Didn't Know

The biggest motivating factor in training is you. To be a good teacher, remember three things: consistency, clarity, and compassion.

Be consistent. Use one familiar command in similar situations, and encourage everyone involved with your dog to do the same. If two people have different expectations, your dog won't know who to believe.

Be clear in your communication. Doglish, not English: stand tall and over-enunciate.

Be compassionate and praise a lot.

Name

Your first goal is to get your dog to alert to his name: "Name," check in. "Name," check in. There are two sure-fire techniques to use.

Hand Signals
Does your dog jump wildly when he hears the cup shake? If so, look up to the ceiling and don't look down until all four are firmly planted on the floor. Teach everyone this Four Paw Rule.

The first is treat cups. Place some broken-up treats in a plastic cup. Make multiple cups and place them all around your house. Every time you walk by the cup, shake it and call out your dog's name. When he looks to you with all four paws on the floor, say, "Good boy!" and offer him a treat.

The second way to make sure your dog alerts on his name is to take him into a quiet room once a day and, standing tall, call out his name. When your eyes connect, hold your stare until he looks away, then praise him and leave the room. Don't overdo this one. *Once* a day in a quiet setting is enough.

Name, Let's Go

After you've got your dog to focus on his name, it's time to teach him proper following manners. With your dog on leash, hold the end loop firmly or secure it around your waist if you're using the Teaching Lead. Now walk forward confidently. The second your dog forges ahead call, "Name, Let's Go" and turn away from him promptly without thought or encouragement. Continue to do this until your dog figures out that you're the one to watch.

Grrr

Beware of the dog that stops dead in his tracks. This fellow is trying to control the rhythm of your walk. Don't hesitate; keep walking, praising only when he walks with you.

No Sir (Or Ma'am)

This is one of the most important commands your dog must learn. I know, it's obvious, but most dogs aren't clear on the true meaning of this word. Some hear "No" so much that they think it's their name!

To teach your dog to obey No Sir (or Ma'am), you must first teach him the definition. Here's how:

➤ With your dog in the next room, place a plate of cookies on the floor.

➤ Put your dog on a leash and bring him into the room. Approach the plate.

➤ The very second your dog notices the plate, snap the leash back firmly and say, "No Sir (or Ma'am)."

➤ Walk by the cookies.

➤ If your dog shows any interest whatsoever, repeat the procedure.

➤ Play this game the next day, with some cheese or steak perhaps.

➤ Keep the corrections focused on the deed. After your dog turns his attention back to you, praise him, and continue your walk.

Pretty soon your dog will see a plate on the floor and turn his nose toward the sky: *"I don't see anything!"*

Bet You Didn't Know

Timing is almost everything; attitude is the rest of it. Corrections should occur the second your dog starts to contemplate a mischievous deed, not after the fact. If he's already downed the cookies, you're too late! Know how you can tell what your dog is thinking? Watch his ears. They're the canine equivalent of antenna.

Now you're ready to start using No Sir around everyday distractions. Try it with one of your snacks. Keeping your dog on a leash, sit in a chair. Have an Oreo, a potato chip or perhaps a piece of cheese. If his nose shifts in your direction, snap the leash back and say "No Sir!" Do this without making eye contact.

Sarah Says

There is a strong connection between the leash snap and the No Sir command. The two of them must happen simultaneously for any long-term, off-leash value. The snap alone works, but if you forget to say "No Sir," your dog will have no idea what you're talking about when he's off leash.

No, you're not teasing him. He must learn that not all food is his. He'll be more pleasant at dinner time, calmer during the kid's snack time, a welcome party guest, and a fine addition at neighborhood barbecues!

After you've got the food thing clear, try using No Sir whenever your dog is paying too much attention to the countertops. If he's off-lead, stamp your foot as you say "No Sir!"

Perfected that? Now it's time to hit the road. Whenever your dog alerts to a bicyclist, a jogger, a friend from the neighborhood, or a car, give his leash a quick tug as you say "No Sir!" Immediately refocus his attention with "Let's Go," and praise.

Sit and Stay

Sit is the first of the stationary commands, and it's necessary to learn in order to get to the fun stuff. Teach it by using this common sense approach: Give the command "Sit" once before anything your dog perceives as positive:

➤ Meals

➤ Treats or toys

➤ Pats

➤ Greeting after an absence

Give the Sit command once, gently positioning your dog if he doesn't listen. Avoid repeating yourself, as repeating isn't cool in any language. After one week, gradually taper off the positive rewards, but keep the praise going.

Next, introduce the Stay command. At first, say it while standing at your dog's side: "Stay," then pause–2–3, and release with "Okay!" Now tell your dog to "Stay" and pivot directly in front of him. Return to his side and release with "Okay!" As your dog catches on, increase your distance and add some distractions (you can hop around or make funny sounds—it'll be fun).

Hand Signals
Use hand signals with your commands from the start. For Sit, swing your open right hand from your dog's nose to your eyes, as if you're scooping his attention toward you.

Wait and Okay

The second stationary command, this one's a real prize. It means to stand still and wait to be released. First you must teach the dog that Wait means stop, stand and focus; then he learns Okay means it's all right to move. It's permission training, step two. It's a self control thing. You teach it like this:

➤ Pick any threshold in your home.

➤ Holding your dog to your side on leash, walk to this threshold.

➤ Stop abruptly as you reach the threshold and say "Wait."

➤ If he bolts anyway, pull him back behind your heels and repeat "Wait!"

➤ Repeat the pull back as often as necessary until he pauses and looks to you.

➤ After he's checked in, say "Okay" and lead him through.

Now you're ready for the big time! Go to your main doorway. Prepare yourself as previously, holding the leash back behind your body. Command "Wait" just before you open the door. If your dog bolts, be ready. Snap him back behind your feet and repeat "Wait." When he does, say, "Okay" as you lead him through.

After you've mastered the front door, try the car. Take your dog to your car and instruct him to Wait as you open the door. If he lunges, snap him back, refusing to let him in until he looks to you for permission.

Hand Signals
A flat palm flashed quickly in front of your dog's nose is the hand signal for Wait and an upbeat flash outward is used for Okay.

Bet You Didn't Know

Ever hear of the *fishbowl effect*? It happens when bossy dogs are confined in a car. They naturally assume this is part of their territory. The resulting jumping and barking can be a real nuisance, not to mention a true danger. If this sounds too familiar, you must regain control of your car. If your dog controls the car, he controls you, making trick training difficult, if not impossible!

At this point your dog should perk up every time he hears you say "Wait." Start using it whenever you want your dog to stand still: talking to friends, visiting the veterinarian, or as a preliminary step to more advanced training.

Down

The last of our stationary commands, this one is a beauty. So applicable and so useful. Initially this exercise can be a real bear to teach, but if you build it around positives your dog will catch on in no time.

➤ Take out a favorite toy or treat.

➤ Give the command "Sit," then take the treat and hold it on the ground slightly in front of him.

➤ Let your dog puzzle over the predicament, but don't release the prize or say anything until his elbows touch the floor.

➤ As he lowers himself, say "Down," then praise, reward, and release him.

Sarah Says
Your dog will learn best if you progress from limited distractions to more stimulating areas.

Continue this exchange for anything positive. After three days, say "Down" from a standing position, adding your hand signal, which is a downward drop of your left hand. Continue the reward exchange for another three days, then begin to phase out the object reward, relying solely on your verbal praise.

Excuse Me

This command must be said with an ounce of attitude. It's a good one when your dog is under foot, crosses in front of you, or swings to the wrong side when you're walking.

What's the point, you ask? Well in dogland, subordinates watch out for their leaders. So to answer your question, Excuse Me communicates leadership; it demands respect. So now a question for you: How often does your dog *naturally* watch out for you? How often does he automatically get up and move aside when you pass? Are some of you laughing? You're not alone.

New rules, however. If your dog is in your way, say "Excuse Me," and move him to one side. No stepping over. No walking around. No changing direction. If he won't move, shimmy your feet beneath him or nudge him aside with your knees. Don't renavigate an inch.

Grrr
A dog must learn the *three-inch exclusion zone.* Unless invited in, he must respect this space between you and him. Crowding is a sign of dominance or insecurity; neither are good for long-term relationships.

To get some extra mileage from this word, use it whenever your dog leans against you (full bodied or with a toy), crosses in front when you're trying to walk, or blocks your path when you are trying to leave a room or use the stairs.

The Least You Need to Know

➤ Dogs don't understand English. They have their own unique communication system which is based on eye contact, body language, and tone. To be a good teacher, you must speak their language.

➤ Attitude is everything! Dogs respect confidence, so don't forget to strut your stuff when you're with them.

➤ If your dog's a bit rusty on his obedience you'll need to find the right collar and leash to get you started. Training collars come in three types and finding the correct one ensures an easy enjoyable training process.

➤ Trick training, whether useful or fun, requires a quick, enthusiastic response to basic commands. Make sure your dog learns the Magic Seven before you press him for more difficult feats.

➤ The Magic Seven foundation commands aren't just for tricks. Use them conversationally throughout the day, linking them to positive outcomes to keep your dog's spirits high.

➤ Most of all, have fun!

Whatever Makes Their Tails Wag

Chapter 3

In This Chapter

➤ How does the building block approach make trick training easy?

➤ The many ways to motivate and reward your dog

➤ The secrets of clicker training

When I was growing up, when you didn't understand someone everyone just said, "Well, whatever floats their boat." At fifteen, however, I was always putting my own spin on things, so what did I—the ardent dog lover—say? "Whatever makes their tail wag." Now, a decade and a half later, that little saying is coming in pretty handy.

In this chapter we'll talk about teaching approaches and discover what gets that dog of yours going, from clicker training to the point system. It's a new age of dog training out there and there's so much to explore! Also on the menu is how to use reinforcements to encourage quick responses and happy participation.

The Building Block Approach

When teaching fun and useful tricks, keep your training sessions short and sweet; no more than five minutes. Repeat the sessions one to four times during the day. Your dog *will* learn, as long as you're positive and use the *building block approach*.

"What's the building block approach?" you ask. It's fairly simple. Each new routine will have steps to follow, and you need to perfect each step before moving on to the next. Let's look at jumping through a hoop. The first step is to get your dog to jump over a low broom when he hears the command Over. The next step is to let him get accustomed to the hoop at ground level; as he walks through he should hear the command Through.

Step three is to put the two together by holding the hoop above the broom, and step four is when you ask your dog to jump through the hoop alone. So we have four steps. Because your dog can't master an entire routine in five minutes, you'll need to isolate each step and build on your dog's successes. There we have it folks…the building block approach.

When Praise Alone Won't Do

You might be lucky enough to have the rare dog that responds to your desires just to make you happy. "You want me to fetch you a soda instead of resting here by this sunny window? Where's the fridge?" Then again, you might not.

Sarah Says
The first time your dog perfects a routine, offer him a *jackpot* and a load of praise. Jackpots are a special treat or toy, or a handful of the rewards you use for training, to let your dog know how psyched you are that he got it together!

I'm sure many of my clients are reading this with their jaw on the floor, recalling my classroom lectures about the mortal sins of using treats with training. That rule still counts with Obedience work (where food is forbidden in the competition ring), but trick training is another matter. The word "trick" itself conjures up visions of magic, laughter, and fun, and while you're enjoying the fruits of your training, your dog shouldn't be left out.

What you'll use to entice your dog will depend on your dog. First you must decide exactly what makes his tail wag hardest. Is it food? Toys? You?

To help you find out, have two people other than yourself stand three feet apart. Give one person the dog's favorite toy. Give the other the packaging of his favorite treats. Now position yourself three feet from them and have someone else let your dog into the room while everyone tries to entice him. Who does he go to? If you're unsure of the results, have a retrial. Have several. Pretty soon the choice will be undeniable. And don't be disappointed if he didn't run to you. Most dogs, like spouses and children, put their parents last.

You

If he did come to you, your heartfelt enthusiasm will be sufficient to encourage your dog through most of his training routines. This is not to say that you can't slip in a favorite treat or toy now and then, but it won't be a requirement to get him to work. Regardless of his devotion, end all sessions with a good game.

Food

Does your dog live for food? He's in the majority. Now you'll need to figure out what your dog likes best. Strive for low-cal rewards that are easy and quick to swallow. Whenever possible, I use Cheerios (the breakfast cereal). If your dog turns up his nose, however, you'll need to find something a bit more tempting.

Most dogs would fly like a rocket for dried hotdog bits. To see what yours thinks, cut a slice off a hotdog and nuke it in the microwave for sixty seconds. After letting it cool, offer it up. Yes? If not, you'll have to continue your search.

Grrr
Treats should be small and easy to swallow, so your dog won't take too long or fill up. Don't treat your dog when he's not having lessons, or it won't seem as exciting.

Whatever food you end up with, cut it into small pieces so that when you're training, he won't fill up.

Toys

Have you ever seen a dog that lives for a toy? It's quite remarkable and is like a child and a security blanket. If this is your pal, your job is easy. To encourage responsiveness all you'll need to do is control the toy. Get your dog accustomed to hearing a phrase like, "Where's your ball?" or, "Get your toy!" so that you can use it to reinforce his efforts.

Now that you've discovered what really revs your dog's engine, use it. As he improves he'll respond just for the fun of it, but for the learning process you'll have to egg him on with whatever makes his tail wag!

Clicker Training

I was first introduced to clickers at a three-day seminar in Phoenix, Arizona. Apparently I was late on the scene, so if you don't know what a clicker is, don't feel bad. In technical terms a *clicker* is a small handheld device that is used to "mark" behaviors when they occur. In everyday English, it's a small box that you use to make a distinct clicking sound at the same time you hand out your dog's favorite reward. Each time he does what you want him to do, you can let him know quickly and clearly. Am I confusing you? Let's take a closer look.

A clicker

When you press the metal strip inside a clicker, it lets out a distinct click, which is quickly followed by a treat or toy. For example, if you were teaching your dog to kiss, you would click the second he gave a kiss, then quickly offer his favorite reward. Timing is everything with the clicker, as your dog will know the sound soon after you introduce him to it. Here's how to get started:

Sarah Says
Using clickers is optional. It's one *very* fun way to teach tricks, but you also can snap your fingers, make a clicking sound with your tongue, or use a sharp, happy word like "Yes!" to let your dog know he's on the right track.

➤ Buy a clicker (you can use the form at the back of this book to order one).

➤ Line up your dog's favorite treats or toys on a table.

➤ Click and offer the treat or toy and praise.

➤ Repeat this ten times; click and reward (saying "Good dog!" too).

➤ After your dog connects the click with the reward, you're ready to use it to teach your first trick.

Touch This, Touch That

After your dog understands the clicker-reward connection, take a long object such as the end of a kitchen utensil or a pencil tip and hold it out for your dog. The second he touches it with his nose, click and reward. Don't say anything yet, just click and reward until your dog makes the connection.

Teaching your dog to touch things on command lays the foundation for all kinds of tricks.

When your dog figures out that all he has to do to get the treat is to touch the end of the object, begin to introduce the command Touch. Using the same object, hold it to your dog's left and his right. Hold it in front and in back. Up and down. Move it around little by little until your dog follows the pointer like a magnet, gently touching it each time. We'll be using this routine as a building block to many others, so congratulate yourselves—you've just performed your first trick!

With clicker training, getting everything in the right order is important. So it's worth repeating. When teaching your dog with the clicker, keep this sequence in mind:

➤ Click and reward the instant your dog does what you want.

➤ After your dog makes the connection and starts responding voluntarily, introduce a command.

➤ Have your dog repeat the behavior a few times before the click, and reward.

➤ When your dog listens to the command, taper off the use of the clicker.

Grrr
Rule of paw! No clicks should go unrewarded. If you click, you must reward. One click, one reward.

Stand Here, Stand There

Another essential foundation routine is to have your dog stand in a specified spot. This one requires more patience, but once learned it's never forgotten. Here's how to teach it:

➤ Take a blank sheet of regular typing paper and place it near you on the floor. With clicker and treats ready, sit tight until your dog puts his two front paws on the paper. Click, praise and reward.

➤ Pick up the paper, move it a few inches and wait again. You may have to wait a while in the beginning, so be patient. When your dog's front paws hit the paper, click, praise and reward.

➤ In the beginning it won't matter what direction your dog's facing or what position he's in when his front paws hit the paper. But after he gets the idea, start clicking only when your dog's facing you.

Grrr
If your dog mouths the paper or the pointer, try practicing with him at a low energy time and use the No Sir command learned in the previous chapter. Don't introduce too much discipline, however, or your dog won't want to work with you. Click only for responses where your dog's mouth is shut! Selectively rewarding will do the job without disciplining.

➤ After your dog catches on, start using the command Here and pointing to the paper. Click, reward and praise!

➤ When your dog starts responding to your command, move the paper away from you incrementally.

➤ Now go back to the first step (close by your feet), but use a smaller piece of paper, perhaps cutting a few inches off the original.

➤ Your goal is to be able to send your dog across the room to stand on a small business card and give him his trick commands at distance. This is the long-range plan.

The Least You Need to Know

➤ Use the building block approach when introducing new routines to your dog. Mastering small steps helps your dog feel empowered as you progress to more difficult tasks.

➤ Every dog has drives. Some will do back flips for a Milk Bone; others will warm up your car on cold mornings for a few tosses of their favorite toy. Some will even do tricks just to make you smile! Make sure you know what motivates your dog to do his best.

➤ With training, timing is everything. Make sure you time your commands, and your rewards, so it's perfectly clear to the dog what he's supposed to be doing and when he's got it right.

Part 2
Let's Get Physical

I'll level with you: I'm not a huge exercise fan. Oh sure, in my younger days I bounced around the track and cheered with the best of them, but now I'd rather curl up with a good book than squirm around in my spandex pants.

Two months ago, to my surprise (and all those who know me well,) I found myself persuaded to join a fitness class with a friend of mine. After the first two nights I thought I was literally going to fall apart. Everything ached. Then I started to question my diet. Not that I'm a junk food maniac, but that's what fitness does to you—makes you question your old life completely. Then I started to wonder if I complained about a sore back or throbbing knee if I should abort the whole fitness endeavor and return to my old, sedentary life.

Well, here I am eight weeks later, and although I'm no fitness junkie, I'm still with it. So why am I sharing this with you? Because if your dog could tell you his thoughts, he'd have similar comments to make. Getting physical with your dog, especially if he's adjusted to a less than physical way of life, will be a transition. And although your dog will enjoy the extra attention, you can't forget that he's got some adjusting to do, too. Evaluating his diet, recognizing the importance of proper conditioning, and being aware of common sports injuries is necessary to get your dear doggy into the exercise groove.

A Go-Active Health Plan

Because many of the activities in this book require physical exertion, your dog needs a health clearance from your veterinarian. Dogs, being dogs, will do their best to please you, even when they're not feeling well. You need to recognize problems and be sensitive when your dog is under the weather. Also, for those sworn couch potatoes, *you'll* need to start with some proper conditioning before you set your sights on the Broadway lights or sign up to run the Iditarod!

A Clean Bill of Health

What exactly does a clean bill of health mean? For the right answer, I went to a pro: my veterinarian.

Your Veterinarian's Approval

My veterinarian started out with a check list:

➤ **Pulse.** A dog's pulse should be between 60 and 160 beats per minute at rest, depending on their size; smaller dog, faster pulse. A quick listen with a stethoscope (no talking please) will tell if the blood's flowing properly.

➤ **Breathing.** Breathing is one of life's simple pleasures. It's essential for all living things. Your veterinarian will listen to make sure your dog inhales and exhales properly.

➤ **Coat and skin.** Different breeds have different coats. My vet likes to see a coat that's free from parasites and properly oiled. When checking the skin, it's important that it be clear and smooth. Any lumps, loss of hair, discoloration, scales, or pimples are cause for alarm.

Grrr
Dogs should only be bathed once a month. Shampooed too often, their coat will dry out and become brittle.

➤ **Eyes.** A dog's eyes should be free of mucous and hair and not too pink. A glance under the third eyelid will tell if a dog's in good health or if there's an infection or sickness elsewhere in the body.

➤ **Ears.** A dog's ear has a big flap that makes it more likely than ours to gather dirt and moisture—which can cause an infection. Your veterinarian will check the ears to make sure they're clean and your dog can hear what you're saying.

➤ **Teeth.** It's a good idea to brush your dog's teeth. My vet provides me with a kit. He even insisted on one for my cat! An examination of your dog's mouth will tell if his gums are infected or if he's suffering from periodontal disease.

➤ **Paw pads and nails.** A dog's paw pads should be soft, not rough. Avoid wear and tear on concrete or pebbled surfaces and keep your dog clear of broken glass. Your veterinarian will check his nails and cut them if they are too long. Overgrown nails are uncomfortable.

➤ **Bones and tissues.** A proper check-up should include rotation of the major joints to make sure your dog's skeleton is aligned or your puppy's growth plates are developing normally.

➤ **Vaccines.** Your veterinarian also will notify of you of your dog's vaccine schedule. Vaccines are given first during puppyhood and are continued throughout a dog's life.

➤ **A sample, please.** The final thing your veterinarian will want to check is your dog's stool, urine, and blood to make sure nothing alien is floating inside. Bring in a stool sample and don't let your dog pee until *after* his exam!

Home Care

Now that you've got your veterinarian's blessing, it's time to set up a home clinic to keep your dog in shape. Brushes, nail clippers, toothpaste, cotton swabs, monthly medications…these are just some of the paraphernalia you'll use to keep your dog in top condition.

Brushing

Grooming can be your worst nightmare or your best friend. If the thought of brushing your dog troubles you, try this:

➤ Start with a soft-bristled brush.

➤ Call your dog aside happily, giving him a treat when he comes.

➤ Take some peanut butter and rub it on a wall at your dog's nose level.

➤ While he licks it off, say "Stand" and brush gently. Praise too!

➤ Quit while you're ahead and increase the brushing time slowly. Eventually, your dog will consider brush times endearing.

The peanut butter trick makes grooming easy. (The brush is a special tool that pulls out dead hair from the dog's coat.)

Bathing

Everyone has to bathe their dog. To make it a positive experience, lay a towel on the bottom of the sink or tub (for your dog to stand on comfortably without slipping) and spread peanut butter around the edge to occupy your dog while you scrub.

Bet You Didn't Know

The peanut butter trick also works wonders when you must towel dry or wipe a dog's paws. If early association with the activity is positive, your dog will be much easier to handle down the road. If your dog's not a big peanut butter fan, try some soft cheese or chicken or beef broth.

My Nails, Darling

Unfortunately, dogs don't relate to the whole manicure thing the way some women do. I hate to sound redundant, but using treats or peanut butter can calm the most savage beast!

The best nail clipper looks like a guillotine. When clipping, make sure you clip the very tip of the nail, just as it starts to curl. (If your dog has light colored nails, you can see the delicate bood vessel inside; that's the part you want to avoid!) And don't overlook dew claws or hind nails. Though they grow more slowly, they still need your attention. If nails grow too long they can crack, break, or become ingrown. Ouch!

Cut on the dotted line.

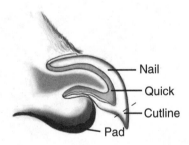

— Nail
— Quick
— Cutline
— Pad

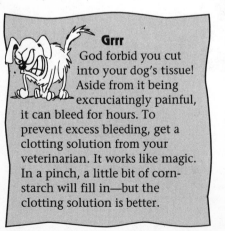

Grrr
God forbid you cut into your dog's tissue! Aside from it being excruciatingly painful, it can bleed for hours. To prevent excess bleeding, get a clotting solution from your veterinarian. It works like magic. In a pinch, a little bit of corn-starch will fill in—but the clotting solution is better.

If your dog's not comfortable having her feet handled, make it a part of your everyday interactions. Handle the feet when giving a treat, petting, or feeding. Tell your dog how wonderful her feet are. Kiss them when she's sleeping. (Okay, you don't have to kiss your dog's feet, but you can.)

If your dog is totally opposed to the clipper, you'll have to do some conditioning work there, too. Let your dog get accustomed to the sound when you're playing or talking to her. Then clip around your dog's paws, without coming into contact. Next, try cutting one nail—just one. Slowly build up her tolerance, one nail at time!

Look at That Face

Dogs don't spend as much time on their looks as you do, but that doesn't mean their facial features should go unnoticed.

Eyes

Soulful, sweet, comic—your dog's eyes tell it all. It's up to you to keep the eyes healthy, bright, and clear. Don't let your dog hang her head out of the car window. Sure, it looks refreshing, but one pebble could knock out an eye for good!

Also, be careful when playing games or practicing tricks that call for the use of a pointy object or stick. Eyes are very tender! Take care of them and take your dog to the doctor if his eyes get tearful, red, swollen, or itchy.

If your veterinarian prescribes eye medication, administer it carefully. Use peanut butter on the fridge or a bowl of broth in a friend's lap to occupy your dog while you medicate him. Place your hand carefully under your dog's chin and pull the lower eye lid down until you see the white part. Squeeze the drops in there.

> **Sarah Says**
> If you have a long-haired breed, carefully clip the hair surrounding the eyes. Better to see you with!

Ears

I'm mesmerized by this body part. I can lull myself into a trance petting ears and it doesn't seem to matter what shape—uprights, floppy, short, or cropped. Dogs seem to love the ear massage, too.

Different dogs require different cleaning schedules, from every couple of weeks to daily. Your dog's activity and the weather also influence the frequency of cleaning. If your dog is an Olympic swimmer, I suggest daily cleaning before bed. In most cases, twice a month is sufficient.

To clean the outer flap, ask your veterinarian to recommend a commercial ear solution that will prevent infection. Soak a cotton swab with the solution and wipe the outer ear flap.

If your dog's ear gets infected, follow the same procedure that was used for medicating the eye. If your dog has drop ears, gently lift the flap and place the medicine where your veterinarian has instructed.

> **Grrr**
> Never, never, never use a Q-tip or poke your finger into your dog's ear. You can do irreparable damage!

Nose

There's not to much to say about the dog's nose. When I was growing up, people used to say you could tell a dog's mood by touching his nose. If it was hot, the dog was sick; too dry, the dog was depressed. The truth is there's no truth to that old wives' tale. A dog's nose can heat up in a warm environment and can dry out when the air is dry. If you want to know if your dog's running a fever, take his temperature—rectal style!

A dog's nose can get discolored. How? Sometimes from the sun or other times it can be an allergic reaction to a food dish or household detergent. In such a case, use a stainless steel bowl and clean with environmentally safe products. And when your dog goes out into the sun, protect that nose with sunblock SPF 45!

Mouth

I have one obsession: It's my teeth. I love brushing, flossing, and going to the dentist. Odd, I know. Based on this, you probably know what I'm going to suggest before I even write it. You must take care of your dog's teeth. Though dogs are less prone to tartar build-up than you are, they're not immune. Sure, they have more concentrated saliva and they chew bones and things, but this doesn't take the place of dental care. Without a little help from their friends (that's you), they'll suffer from tooth decay, cavities, abscesses, periodontal disease, and tooth loss.

Grrr
Avoid human toothpaste; fluoride and dogs don't mix.

To keep your dog's teeth healthy:

➤ Feed dry food. Crunchy is better.

➤ Brush your dog's teeth once a week, using special canine toothpaste. If your dog won't settle for the brush, use your finger.

You can get a toothbrush kit just for dogs.

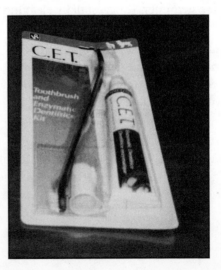

Conditioning, Conditioning

Now that you can rest assured your dog is healthy, you need to make sure he's in top physical condition, or has a program to get him there, before you jump into this new activity regime. Just like humans, pushing your dog too far too fast can lead to trouble.

The Hip Bone's Connected to the Thigh Bone

If you took a look inside your little trickster, you'd see that you're a lot alike. Sure the bones are stacked differently, but they're all there, put together as perfectly as a puzzle. And like us, dogs' bones are glued together with special tissues called ligaments. The place where bones meet each other is called a joint, and its movement and flexibility is controlled by tendons, which connect muscle to bone. Where free-moving joints meet, the ends are protected by a layer of cartilage.

In a perfect world this puzzle would always be the same, but there is no such thing as a perfect world. Each dog in the world has a unique conformation, and understanding your dog's physical strengths and limitations is necessary for training.

Physicalities

If your dog's anything like me, the thought of exercising will send him flying under the covers. Fortunately, however, most dogs aren't like me. They love to run and play and be a part of whatever you're doing. If your dog has not been out for a good run in a long time, you'll need to ease him in slowly. Conditioning for dogs is like conditioning for us—a necessary evil.

Start with conditioning for tricks and obedience. Most of the stunts outlined in this book don't require tremendous amounts of physical exertion. However, if your dog has been off the training wagon for some time, keep the lessons short and upbeat to start: No more than three minutes. He doesn't have to master a trick a day.

Start with tricks that are easy for him to master and that make you laugh. Laughter is great encouragement. You can have practice sessions three times a day if your schedule allows, but short lessons are best.

Conditioning for activities is another thing. Are you pumped up to start racing that dog of yours over every tree and up ladders? Whoa Nellie! Your dog will want to try everything you introduce him to, but is he ready? If your dog can't tell a tree stump from an ottoman, start small. No need to conquer the world in a day.

First, take a couple of weeks to make sure your dog can handle the excitement. Go for half-mile hikes, building the distance over time. A four-month-old pup will run until his legs can't carry him, but all that exercise can

Grrr
Do not jump your puppy higher than the height of his elbow. Also avoid over-feeding your pup. Extra weight can strain developing growth plates!

permanently alter his growing muscles and cause hip problems later in life. I know—teaching your dog new stuff is a lot of fun, but you need to be the parent here and do what is best for your dog.

Never forget the age factor. Growing pups are in the majority where sports injuries are concerned. A young dog's energy and enthusiasm can be quite misleading: They'll want to try everything and give no thought to the consequences. Trauma to bones and joints are caused by overstrenuous activity, slippery footing, or excessive jumping. During your puppy's growth phase—four-and-a-half to nine months—keep his activity level regulated and do not encourage jumping.

Let's talk breeds. Picture a Dachshund: dwarfed-out legs, long body, endearing eyes, and the greatest paddle paws on the planet. Now clear your head and envision a Boxer: upright, statuesque, proud, magnificently angled, and proportioned to a T. No one on the planet would ever ask them both for the same performance. One has legs meant for digging, the other for running. Now go take a look at your dog. What breed or mix of breeds have you got? Sure you may be all hyped for Agility trials, but if your Bulldog Mugs is snoring on the couch, don't plan on taking home any trophies.

Make sure you monitor the activity level of growing puppies.

The Least You Need to Know

➤ Make sure your dog has a veterinarian's health check before beginning training.

➤ What do brushing, bathing, nail clipping, and medicating have in common? They're no fun! But they're a necessary evil—canine style. Stay calm and use goodies and praise to make the process more positive. Never lose your cool.

➤ Conditioning for a dog is like conditioning for a human—there's no avoiding it. If your dog is a sworn couch potato, ease into your new activity regime slowly.

➤ Take it easy with puppies. Their boundless energy can cause problems for their growing bones.

Sports Injuries

In This Chapter

➤ The common causes of limping, and how to deal with them

➤ What do to if your dog goes into shock

➤ How to transport an injured dog to the veterinarian

Activity training, whether it be the simplest tricks, such as wagging the tail, or jumping an Agility wall, requires movement. And with all movement there is the possibility of injury. From a torn ligament or cartilage to a slipped spinal disc, you must learn to read your dog's signs because he can't talk to you.

If your dog has an accident during a workout, you need to stay cool. If you lose it, he'll get nervous and go to pieces. Be a rock of confidence. Be mentally tough. Organize. Think. If need be, get him to the hospital as quickly and carefully as possible.

Let's take a look at some of the things that can happen to your active dog, what causes them, and how to cope.

Limping

This is the most common result of a sports injury. Your job is to find out what is causing your dog to limp and which body part is in trouble. To figure out just where the pain is centralized:

➤ Watch your dog. When he's standing still it should be obvious which leg is being favored.

➤ Now watch him walk. He'll take a shorter step on his injured leg. His head also may bob up and down to compensate for the pressure he's trying to keep off his hurt limb.

➤ To pinpoint the specific injury site, carefully rub your hands along your dog's joints and note any muscle tenderness.

Limping is the most common result of a sports injury.

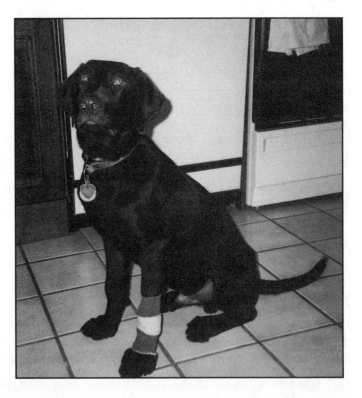

➤ If you're still puzzled, gently flex and rotate your dog's joints.

➤ Now check for discoloration and swelling and take your dog's temperature with a rectal thermometer. (Oh joy!)

Bet You Didn't Know

Even the most beloved pet may bite when in pain or confused. If he doesn't bite you, he'll probably go for his veterinarian or one of the technicians, so restrain your dog for their sake, please.

The simplest restraining technique requires a bandanna or a rope.

➤ Fold the bandanna into a long band.

➤ Drape the center of the band across the top of your dog's nose.

➤ Cross the two ends underneath your dog's chin.

➤ Tie the end securely behind your dog's ears

➤ Check the crossing point underneath. If it's too loose, your dog will pull it off; if it's too tight, you'll choke your dog.

After you've identified the source of the problem, check the dog's symptoms against the table shown here and follow the treatment plan. Remember that the quicker an injury is diagnosed, the easier it is to treat and the less likely it is your dog will need surgery. That's why it's important to see your veterinarian whenever your dog gets hurt.

Common Sports Injuries

Injury	What Is It?	Causes	Symptoms	Treatment
Sprain	Stretching or laceration of the ligaments, most commonly in the joints	Stretching, a blow, lack of conditioning	Pain over the joint, swelling, lameness, decreased enthusiasm for activity	Rest and more rest; ice the area 20 minutes per hour for the first three hours; avoid pain medication, as it encourages use of the limb, unless recommended by veterinarian
Tendonitis	Inflammation of the tendon	Overuse, too much activity, an accident causing twisting or wrenching	Localized swelling, painful movement, limping	Plenty of rest, splinting may be necessary, stop all activity that puts pressure on the injured area, avoid pain relievers without your vet's recommendation

continues

continued

Injury	What Is It?	Causes	Symptoms	Treatment
Muscle strain	An injured or torn muscle	Over-exertion, a sudden stretch, a blow to the muscle, lack of conditioning unrealistic expectations	Limping, swelling a knotted and tight muscle, tenderness at the injured spot	Rest, cold packs as for sprain
Torn ligament	Tear or laceration to the ligament	Stretching, a blow, lack of conditioning, a knotted or tight muscle	Moderate to severe lameness or complete inability to use the limb, swelling tenderness	Requires immediate veterinary attention, often demands surgical repair to avoid developing scar tissue
Dislocated joint	Joint ruptures and displaces bones	Falling, collision with a hard object such as a wall	Immediate pain inability to use the limb, visible deformity	See your veterinarian immediately; if dog is in shock, treat that first.
Fracture	Broken bone	Severe trauma, such as a fall or a car accident	Pain, refusal to use the limb, bone may protude through the skin	Muzzle the dog, immobilize the limb, take immediately to the hospital; if you suspect internal or spinal injury, place on a board to move; the dog may also experience shock, blood loss, or internal bleeding—address these problems first.

Genetic Skeletal Disorders

Genetic disorders are passed from parent dogs to puppies on blueprints known as genes. *Hip dysplasia,* which mostly occurs in larger dogs, both pure-bred and mixed, is one of these genetic disorders. Normally, the head of the femur (thigh bone) fits into the hip socket and rotates freely as your dog moves around. In a perfect world it would always be so. In a moderately dysplastic dog, however, loose ligaments allow the head of the femur to begin to work free. A shallow cup in the hip socket also contributes to this condition.

Because of this joint laxity, there is abnormal wear and tear on the joint. In time this leads to arthritis in the dysplastic joint.

Mild dysplasia creates slips in motion, discomfort, and instability. When hip dysplasia is severe, it's extremely painful. The X-rays make you cringe. With the femoral head degenerated and practically dislocated, motion is crippled and pain is constant. Your veterinarian will inform you of surgical options.

Bet You Didn't Know

A dog can be born with a predisposition for dysplastic disorders, but you can avoid the worst effects by controlling your dog's diet and avoiding stressful exercise.

If your dog has a skeletal disorder such as hip or elbow dysplasia, I'm sorry. It's a big disappointment for both of you, but what are you going to do? You must deal with it and respect the limitations it will put on training. First, a check list of things you can do:

✔ Neuter your dog. Don't pass on your dog's problem to future generations.

✔ Feed your dog a balanced diet.

✔ Avoid high calorie, rapid growth diets. They can aggravate the disorder. The tissues, bones, and muscles must grow together evenly.

✔ Avoid supplementing the diet, especially with calcium. Ask for your veterinarian's suggestion.

✔ Keep your dog's weight down. Too many pounds on a stressed joint is a bad thing.

✔ Talk to your dog's breeder. They should know of your heartache. If they're responsible, they'll eliminate that breeding combination.

✔ Avoid all contributing environmental factors. Long jogs are no good. Correct jumping habits. Are stairs stressful? Talk to your veterinarian.

✔ Buy cozy bedding. Heating pads too…ah, heaven!

✔ Carpet any area your dog travels frequently. Slippery floors don't provide good traction.

✔ Avoid leaving your dog out in the cold. Keep him in a warm, dry environment, especially at night.

✔ Last, but not least, massage that joint. (Avoid putting pressure on the joint itself.) Get blood flowing to the muscles, especially if your dog is on bed rest.

There is a wonderful exercise for dysplastic dogs: swimming. Not everyone is fortunate to have a pond or pool in the backyard, but if you look hard enough you may be able to find a place nearby where your dog can swim. Long swims and leash walks on turf (no cement) can build the muscles up and slowly build your dog's strength.

If you have a setback and the limping starts again, talk to your veterinarian, and ease off strenuous exercise and training. Start back slowly when you're given the go-ahead. Your dog is physically handicapped. He needs you to take care of him.

Shock

A dog can go into shock if there's a sudden loss of blood, a trauma, or electrocution. Shock is life threatening; it causes blood pressure to drop dramatically, which prevents oxygen from circulating in the body. Without oxygen, the body dies quickly.

A dog in shock shows the following symptoms:

➤ A fast heart rate, as the heart tries to make up for a drop in blood pressure

➤ Rapid breathing, because the body is trying to increase oxygen flow

Sarah Says
Be ready! Place towels and a dog-sized board aside for emergencies.

➤ Dilated pupils and a glaring stare

➤ Unconscious or semiconscious behavior

If you suspect your dog has gone into shock, stay calm, keep him still, and get to the nearest veterinarian immediately.

Transporting an Injured Dog

Transporting a dog who has internal injuries is tricky business. They'll be restless and want to move, and it's your job to make sure they don't. It's best to have someone help you out, so they can drive and you can comfort and restrain your dog. If someone isn't available immediately, however, don't delay in getting your dog to the vet.

If you suspect a broken bone, spinal injury, or internal bleeding, transport your dog on a firm surface such as metal or plywood. Otherwise, placing your dog on a sheet or towel is acceptable. Don't cover his face, as it may completely freak him out.

The Least You Need to Know

➤ With any sort of activity comes the possibility of injury. Because dogs often want to do more than their bodies can handle, you need to put restrictions on their enthusiasm.

➤ The most common sign of injury is limping. The causes of a limp can range from a strained muscle to a fractured bone. Be respectful of your dog's signals.

➤ A severe accident can send your dog into shock, which can be fatal if not treated promptly. Dogs in shock *must* see a veterinarian.

➤ Educate yourself in recognizing, treating, and transporting an injured dog.

Diet: A Dog's Eye View

There is more to a fun-loving, happy dog than interaction and training. You need to learn about keeping your dog healthy and well-balanced on the inside, and it starts with a good diet.

I have to admit, I was fairly ignorant about dog foods before I started working as a dog trainer. "A little of this, a little of that" was the stated dog food in my house while growing up. Poor Shawbee, my childhood dog, had a lot of gas to contend with from her irregular fare. Over the years I've learned a lot about dog nutrition. And I'll tell you, it's been a major revelation.

What's in Dog Food?

A good diet is like setting a sturdy foundation before you start building your house. If you don't do it, you could have the finest training regime in history, but your dog won't live up to his fullest potential.

All dog foods aren't the same. Like books and people, you can't judge the contents by what you see on the cover. To pick the right food you'll need to consider (who else?) your dog: his age, breed, and lifestyle.

Dog foods do have certain things in common. To pass regulatory standards, they must contain six essential elements: protein, fat, carbohydrates, vitamins, minerals, and water. But that's where the similarities usually end. The makers of dog foods diverge on what ingredients are used to reach the *minimum daily requirement* (MDR). For example, some use soy (a vegetable protein) to meet the daily protein requirement, while others use animal protein. Let's look at the essentials one at a time.

Sarah Says
As you learn about dog foods and check out a variety of brands, you'll discover that foods that cost more aren't always best.

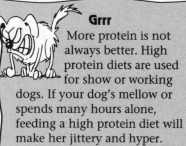

Grrr
More protein is not always better. High protein diets are used for show or working dogs. If your dog's mellow or spends many hours alone, feeding a high protein diet will make her jittery and hyper.

Protein

Protein is the most expensive ingredient in dog foods. Its source often determines the quality of the food. Animal sources are superior. Unfortunately, there's not enough meat around to satisfy all the pet dogs in the world, so we have come up with substitute food: vegetable protein. The difference between vegetable and animal protein? Vegetable is often harder to digest and more of it has to be consumed to meet the dog's needs. More food equals more stool. The moral of the story is: Find a food that uses more animal protein and requires smaller rations to meet the MDR.

Carbohydrates

Some manufacturers meet the MDR for protein by using primarily vegetable matter. Vegetable sources of protein also contain high levels of carbohydrates; not a bad diet for humans, but what's good for humans isn't always good for dogs. The reason we digest carbohydrates well is that we start digestion in our mouths, chewing and breaking down the food as it goes. Dogs don't chew, they gulp, and their digestion doesn't begin until the food gets into their stomach.

Why is this important? Foods high in carbs can cause digestive problems in dogs, such as bloating, upset stomach, constipation, and too much stool. Make sure you pick a diet that contains more animal protein than vegetable protein. How? Read the label and select a food that has two or more animal sources of protein listed in the first five ingredients.

Bet You Didn't Know

Many dogs are allergic to the grains found in dog food. The most common allergies are to corn, wheat, and soy. Certain grains also may contain fertilizer residue, which can cause an allergic reaction. If your dog refuses to eat his food or his digestion seems abnormal in any way, consult your veterinarian. Save the labels from your dog's food. This will help in identifying possible aggravating ingredients.

Fats

Please don't ever buy fat-free dog food. I know it sounds tempting, but your dog needs fat to keep her skin and coat healthy and to transport things around on the inside. Used in the proper moderation, fat will give your dog energy and keep her cool when it's warm and warm when it's cool.

However, fat can be a funny thing. For one, it spoils quickly. If you're feeding your dog a natural diet make sure you respect the expiration date. Rancid fat can lead to a whole slew of health problems.

Vitamins and Minerals

Have you ever wondered what vitamins exactly do and why they're necessary for good health? Vitamins do two things:

➤ They unlock nutrients from food.

➤ They provide energy.

The need for vitamins varies depending on your dog and his lifestyle. The average bag of dog food, however, doesn't take this into consideration. The truth is the MDR was set for laboratory Beagle-type dogs. Take that into account, along with the fact that vitamins are a rather unstable lot, easily destroyed by light and heat, and you'd be wise to invest in a good vitamin supplement. Ask your veterinarian for a suggestion.

Vitamin deficiencies can lead to poor growth, digestive disorders, elimination problems, stool eating, a weak immune system, greasy and stinky coats, Addison's Disease (thyroid malfunction), aggression, timidity, and sterility. Not a pretty list!

Minerals are a lot like their cohorts vitamins. They help the body maintain its normal daily activities, such as circulation, energy production, and cell regeneration. Although mineral deficiencies are not that uncommon, do not supplement your dog's diet unless directed by your veterinarian. That's because too many minerals can cause health problems.

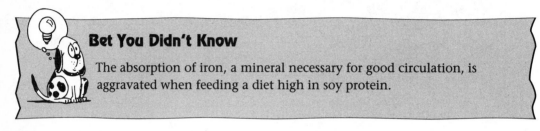

Bet You Didn't Know

The absorption of iron, a mineral necessary for good circulation, is aggravated when feeding a diet high in soy protein.

Water

Did you know that your dog can live three weeks without food, but will die within days without water? Water is necessary for all digestive processes as well as temperature regulation, nutrient absorption, and as a transportation medium, shipping things between organs and out of the body.

Make sure clean water is always available for your dog.

How much water your dog will need depends on his physical activities and the type of food he eats. Panting is your dog's way of sweating. If your dog is sweating, he needs a drink. Dry food also encourages thirst. On the other hand, canned food or home-cooked diets contain more water and require less to rinse and wash down.

Choosing Your Dog's Diet

Deciding on a diet for your dog is no small order. Commercial, dry, canned, home-cooked; the choice is yours, and it isn't an easy one. Every diet doesn't suit every dog, so be a conscientious shopper. Let's take a look at each option.

Commercial Foods

Here are four constants to help you make your selection:

➤ Look for the AAFCO (American Association of Feed Control Officials) stamp of approval.

➤ Note the suggested daily ration. Is it realistic?

➤ Eliminate foods causing weight loss; loose, smelly stools; or poor coat condition.

➤ Respect your dog's judgment. Refusal to touch the food can be attributed to stubbornness, but it's often a sign of spoiled ingredients or allergies.

Next, consider your lifestyle. Do you have a lot of free time to train your dog and engage in high-energy activities? Performance foods with high levels of crude protein provide lots of energy to burn. Puppies also need higher amounts of protein for their growing bodies.

Homemade Diets

There are many pros to a homemade diet for your dog. Followed responsibly, the home diet can be modified for your dog's age, breed distinctions, and individual needs. Personalized diets will enhance your dog's health and vitality.

The drawbacks? These diets can't be fudged. You must commit to preparing *balanced* meals and to shop for products regularly to ensure freshness. If you want to try a homemade diet, please refer to *The Holistic Guide for a Healthy Dog* by Wendy Volhard

Sarah Says
If you want to give your dear dog a bone, please avoid poultry or pork, as they splinter and can have fatal consequences. Beef knuckle and marrow bones are best; just ask your butcher. Parboil them in meat broth to enhance their flavor and kill parasites.

and Kerry Brown, DVM, or *Natural Food Recipes for Healthy Dogs* by Carol Boyle (both from Howell Book House, New York).

Dry vs. Wet Food

What are the differences between dry food and wet food? Cost in shipping and cost to the consumer. Wet food contains 65 percent to 78 percent water; the weight of the can and water increase the cost of shipping.

Wet food is less likely to fill up your dog with grain fillers that he can't really use anyway. Dry food is better for his teeth. No studies have proven either wet or dry to be nutritionally superior. So what it boils down to is that the choice is up to you. Many of the veterinarians I've talked to suggest a combination of the two.

When searching for the right diet, pay close attention to your dog. How is his digestion? Foods with low quality ingredients aren't absorbed well and can give your dog loose stools.

Growing Puppies

I'm a sucker for a young puppy, and though I spoil them as much as possible with kisses and head scratches, I never fudge on their diet. Like a human baby, their digestive systems are very fragile. After weaning they should be kept on the same puppy food for at least eight weeks. If you decide to switch brands of food, do it incrementally over a ten-day period.

There are some key differences between people's diets and puppies' diets. Number one, dogs don't dig fiber. A high-fiber, low-fat diet for a dog of any age could be disastrous. Stool city. Remember dogs are born carnivores, and no New Age fad will change that! Monitor protein and calories if you want to raise a healthy pup. They need more of both, as they're growing mentally and physically.

How much food your puppy will eat depends on his size and weight. Often the portions listed on the back of the bag are exaggerated or estimated for an average dog. And who has an average dog? Not you! To decide on the right amount of food, ask your puppy. Give him as much he'll eat in fifteen minutes and then feed him that much at each meal. If he eats it all, don't offer more. If he doesn't eat anything, don't fret. Dogs are just like that.

Grrr
Overfeeding or sprinkling your puppy's diet with table scraps is a bad thing. Puppies who obsess over food and mealtimes are likely to become pudgy and fat. This is bad for the growth of their bones and muscles and is likely to cause developmental problems down the road.

How often you feed your puppy will depend on his age and your time schedule. I like to feed a young pup (one that's under twelve weeks) four times a day: 7 a.m., 12 noon, 4 p.m., and 10 p.m. I know, I know…lots of stool, lots of stool. But this is how I am.

After twelve weeks I phase out the late night feeding and continue three meals a day until my puppy stops eating one of those meals or reaches six months (whichever comes first). At this point I can rest assured that my pup's stomach can retain the food for longer periods of time. Adapt your schedule to your puppy's needs.

Puppies need to eat special puppy food.

Overweight Dogs

Putting on extra pounds can happen at any time in a dog's life, although it most often occurs in old age. Metabolism slows, and so does the interest in exercising. Fortunately, we live in an age of low-cal dog food that is perfectly balanced for the sedentary dog. Add a healthy walk or two daily, and your dog will be swinging those hips around the neighborhood in no time!

Sarah Says
Here's a quick check to see if your dog's got one too many layers. Stand him up and feel his ribs. If you're having trouble finding them, it's time for a diet!

Special Situations

As your dog ages, he'll need a different balance of nutrition to keep him going. Like us, older dogs need fewer calories. In addition, because the digestive process takes longer in old dogs, you may want to feed smaller meals more often.

Speak to your veterinarian about an appropriate diet for your aging pal. Some dogs have specific ailments that require a prescription diet. Your veterinarian will guide you in your selections and provide an appropriate food to keep your dog well. These diets will have a guaranteed analysis that breaks down each ingredient to ensure you're getting the identical food sources in every bag or can.

The Least You Need to Know

➤ More protein isn't always better. Only use high protein diets if you have a high performance dog!

➤ When buying commercial foods, make sure they have the AAFCO stamp of approval.

➤ Water is vital for survival. Provide clean water in a stainless steel dish and change it regularly.

➤ Many dogs have allergies. If your dog suffers from food allergies, work with your veterinarian to pinpoint the aggravating ingredient and regulate his diet.

➤ Puppies and older dogs have special nutritional needs. Look for foods made just for them, and adjust their feeding schedules as needed.

Part 3
Abracadabra

Trick training, whether you're doing it for the kids, to entertain the neighbors, or just for fun, involves a little magic. But don't tell the neighbors! To see a certifiable trick dog in action is a true wonder. Imagine seeing a dog get shot (by a finger, not a gun) and collapse on the floor in a dead heap. Now go and check out your dog. Can you see him bringing you a soda from the fridge and fetching your slippers? Better yet, can you imagine your dog being psyched about doing your bidding?

Welcome to the art of trick training, where the paw is quicker than the eye! In this section I'll explain each trick in an easy-to-digest format, allowing you to read and understand the process before introducing it to your dog.

Although the task of teaching your dog anything may sound monumental, trick training, when broken down step by step, is as easy as walking the dog.

Fun and Simple Tricks

In This Chapter

➤ The classic Paw trick, with six variations

➤ Playing dog style soccer

➤ Teaching Hide and Seek and Catch Me, the great energy burners

Remember in high school when you showed up in class to discover that instead of a lecture it was a film day? Your brain let out a big sigh of relief, because it knew the hard work was over for the day. Well brain, you can let out a sigh, because the tricks and games in this chapter are easy to master. Some games are designed to burn energy and are good to play when your dog is full of beans. Other tricks are just for fun, and when your dog catches on he'll want to practice as much as you.

The Classic Paw, with Variations

Nothing like starting with a classic. Some dogs are naturally predisposed to this action; so much so that you're probably wondering how to teach No Paw, but we'll get to that later.

After you've mastered the Paw, you can really start being creative. For those of you new to this, get your dog (on a leash if he's antsy), some favorite treats, and go into a quiet room.

Hand Signals
Stretch out your hand, as if to shake paws.

➤ Kneel or sit in front of your dog.

➤ Command "Sit." Position if necessary, and praise.

➤ Using a thumb, press your dog's shoulder muscle gently until his front leg lifts.

➤ Shake his paw warmly, then treat and praise.

➤ After you've got the hang of it and his leg lifts easily, start using the command "Paw" and giving him the hand signal before pressing his muscle (if you still need to).

Say Thank You

Hand Signals
Extend your hand to the dog with your palm up.

This is a real charmer. And after your dog learns the signal, performing this trick is a piece of cake. Give the command "Say Thank You" as you extend your hand to your dog with the palm up. Praise and give him a treat. Now get a human pal to help you out. As they extend a hand and command, "Say Thank You," encourage your dog to offer his paw to your friend. Now you're ready to spread your dog's good manners everywhere!

Other One

Hand Signals
Stretch our your hand to the specified paw.

As your dog catches on you'll notice that he favors either his left or right paw. To prevent having a one-dimensional dog, teach Other One.

➤ Ask "Paw" and lovingly praise your dog.

➤ Now extend your hand to the other paw and say, "Other One."

➤ If your dog lifts his favored paw, use a sound such as "Ep, ep" and repeat your original request, while you put pressure on the muscle of the other paw.

➤ When your dog lifts the other paw, praise, treat, and give him a big hug!

Sarah Says
When teaching tricks, speak clearly, directing your words to your dog, and give each command only once.

Left Paw, Right Paw

By using Other One to get your dog to pay attention to which hand you extend, you can pull off a trick that makes it seem as if your dog can tell his right paw from his left, the little genius!

While in a quiet room, decide which paw your dog gives most frequently; here we'll say it's the left paw. Exaggerate the hand signal as you hold your hand to his left side and say, "Left paw." Praise and offer a treat. Do three lefts, so your dog gets plenty of good reinforcement. If by chance your dog swaps and offers a right paw, say, "Ep, ep, ep, not yet" and wait to reward until the left paw is offered.

Hand Signals
A typical high five, brought down to your dog's level.

Now for the other paw. Exaggerate your hand signal toward the right side and say "Right Paw." Your dog will probably try the left paw. If he does, say "Ep, ep, Other One." Show him physically if you have to. Practice three rights, then quit for now.

The next time you go to practice, start with Right Paw, accentuating your signal. Help your dog out if you must. Do three rights, then three lefts, accentuating the left signal. Soon your dog will catch on and you can mix it up: two rights, two lefts, two rights, one left, one right, and so on. Vary the pattern each time and keep these mind puzzler sessions short. You'll also notice that your dog becomes clued in to your body language, and you can exaggerate the hand signal less and less.

High Five

Okay hot shot, gimme five! This one is easy to teach and dogs love it.

Hold your hand, palm out, at the same height you normally ask for paw. If the command "High Five" gets a puzzled look, then say "Paw" to request the action, and "High Five" as the dog's paw makes contact with your hand. Drop the Paw command when your dog makes the connection. Slowly lift your hand higher to accentuate the High Five.

Grrr
When asking for the High Five, stay within your dog's height capabilities. Don't encourage jumping. High Five is a three-paws-on-the-floor trick.

Give me five, and keep it high!

Go for Ten

An extension of the High Five, Go for Ten involves two hands and two paws. When asking "Go For Ten," keep your hands at about the level of your dog's head. Any higher will encourage jumping.

Remember that some dogs simply can't sit up on their hind legs. You'll know if your dog can't do this trick. So what? You love him anyway!

The High Five Jig

High Five-Low Five-No Five-Shake! I first made up this little jig to play with my niece and nephew, but who's to say dogs won't love it just as much? The goal is to have a good rhythmic movement, but start out slow and you can work up to it.

Sarah Says
Another cool take-off on Paw is Introduce Yourself or Say Hello. Teach your dog the basic Paw, then just cue the same action on another command.

➤ High Five: hold your hand high.

➤ Low Five: hold your hand low.

➤ No Five: purposely miss your dog's paw.

➤ Shake: extend your hand for a paw.

Ever polite, your pooch can introduce herself all around.

Remedies for the Three-Legged Dog

Is your dog too paw expressive? It happens to the best of them. If your dog constantly paws, you have two options: ignore or use a mild correction. Ignoring is self-explanatory. If that doesn't work, try one of the following corrections:

➤ Keep a Short Tab (a very short loop of leash) on your dog (buy one at a pet supply store or use the order form in the back of the book) and snap it downward while saying, "Not Now."

➤ Walk away.

➤ Use your "Ep, ep, ep" sound and command "Sit."

Dogs usually paw because they want something: a treat, a toy, or attention. Avoid giving in to your dog's pestering! You're just teaching him that it works. Wait for more mannerly behavior, such as sitting quietly or lying down, before you give the dog what he wants.

Snoopy Soccer

You'll need one or more players (plus your dog), and an empty plastic soda bottle or a ball for each person and one for the dog. Most dogs love to play with a ball or soda bottle, wrestling and knocking it around with their feet. They also love to use their mouth, which is fine if you just want to mess around. If you're planning on teaching the next four-legged soccer star, however, I suggest you get an indestructible ball made especially for dogs.

This is a goal-oriented game. Here's how to play:

➤ Get your dog interested in the bottle or ball by knocking it around gently.

➤ Interact in random patterns around a field.

➤ When your dog seems focused on this interaction, set up a six-foot wide goal. Use trash cans, poles, or anything else you happen to have handy.

➤ Encourage your dog by saying "Goal" as you kick the bottle or ball toward the goal.

➤ Now for the clicker training we talked about in Chapter 3: Kick the ball or bottle to your dog and say "Goal." Click and offer a treat for the slightest movement toward the goal.

➤ In the beginning, click and reward all movements toward the goal. Slowly space out the rewards, encouraging your dog further toward the goal before you reinforce him.

Grrr
Be careful of your dog's face when kicking things around. If you're just playing soccer to fool around, use two balls and kick the one your dog's not playing with.

➤ Now it's time to go for the goal. Kick the bottle or ball toward your dog three feet in front of the goal and command "Goal!"

➤ The second your dog crosses the line with the bottle or ball, click and reward him!

➤ Now try passing the bottle or ball at farther distances from the goal. Pretty soon you can introduce him to the team!

Get your dog interested in the ball, then watch her go for the goal.

Hide and Seek

This is a great game and also reinforces that indispensable Come command. You need one to four players and a treat cup, and your dog needs to know his name and the Come command. Stay also comes in handy.

Start with this game inside, one-on-one. While your dog's occupied, go into an adjoining room with a treat cup. Call out his name and shake the cup. When you hear him running say "Come" clearly. Praise him, offer a treat, and let him return to whatever he was doing.

After your dog aces this routine, increase the level of difficulty. Call him from two rooms away; but still be in sight, not hard to find. After a couple of days of hiding in plain sight around the house and calling from room to room, go into the adjoining room and hide behind a chair. Increase the difficulty of your hiding places and the distance from your dog as he catches on.

You found me now!

Now you can start playing hide and seek as a team sport. If your dog knows a solid Stay, this is where it helps. Leave your dog in a Stay while you and another teammate or two hide (start off with easy-to-find hiding places). Decide who will call the dog first. After the dog is praised by the first person, have the second person give a holler.

Grrr
If you make your hiding spots too hard too soon, your dog will lose interest fast.

After your dog catches on to this game, you can increase the difficulty of your hiding places and add another teammate. Eventually you two-legged geniuses can play a game to see who gets found first and who gets found last.

Catch Me

I've always hated games that involve people chasing dogs, especially when that game involved a coveted laundry item. Games that encourage your dog to focus on and follow you, however, are a real prize when it comes to training and having fun. These games also reinforce the extinction of bad habits, such as nipping and jumping. Here's how to play:

You need one or two players and a dog toy. Your dog needs to know Sit, Wait, Down, Stay, Okay, and No Sir/Ma'am.

➤ Turn and face your dog from about three to six feet away.

➤ Say "Catch Me," then turn and run.

➤ After a few feet, pop back to face your dog and command "Sit."

➤ Say "Okay" and "Catch Me," and run again.

➤ Pop back, turn, and give another stationary command such as "Wait."

➤ Follow each command with "Okay, Catch Me."

➤ Vary your commands and keep the game short, just one or two minutes.

➤ When you use the word Stay, back away from your dog slowly, then say "Okay, Catch Me" to continue.

➤ When you're through, tell your dog "Okay" and give him a favorite toy.

I know I'll catch some slack for writing about this game. People are always asking if high-energy games encourage mouthing and jumping. My response? If it escalates the dog's bad behavior uncontrollably, leave it out. If your dog enjoys the game and you can curb naughtiness with a sharp "No Sir," then go for it. Catch Me is a fun activity and sharpens your dog's responsiveness to stationary commands.

The Least You Need to Know

➤ The simplest Paw trick can translate into a whole menu of fun routines. From Thank You to High Five, your dog will be a welcome guest at everything from football rallies to tea parties.

➤ Obedience games are great energy burners. If you've got a hot tamale, a game or two a day can keep energy at a manageable level.

➤ Hide and Seek is a fun energy burner and reinforces the command Come.

Mood Swings

Here's a fine display of canine emotion. When your dog can act out each mood with style, you're really on your way to pleasing audiences everywhere. From happy to sad to doggone tired, teaching your dog these tricks is no small accomplishment.

Happy (Wag Your Tail)

This one is sooo easy! Say anything you want in a positive, inviting tone, and watch your dog come alive. Whenever I listen to clients complain about their dog, I turn to the dog and say, "Well aren't you the naughtiest, most terrible little monster! What a nuisance you've become." I say it however, in such a sweet, loving voice that it causes every dog to squirm with delight. The owners can't help but fall in love with their adoring (though confused) doggie all over again.

Try the following phrases on for size:

➤ If you're happy and you know it, wag your tail!

➤ Are you happy?

➤ Who's my best girl/boy?

If you're in front of a crowd you can ask really difficult questions and tell your dog that if he agrees, all he has to do is wag his tail. It goes like this: "I'm going to ask you a hard question and if you agree all you have to do is wag your tail. Ready? Would you like everyone to give you a hug?"

Remember, all you have to do to get your dog to wag his tail is speak in the right tone. Practice right now!

Sarah Says
Please notice that although hand signals are described for some tricks, you must first teach your dog how to do the trick before you expect him to respond to a silent signal.

Sarah Says
Some dogs get really addicted to this game. If you can't get your dog to stop licking you or others, you'll need to teach That's Enough. Keep a Short Tab leash on your dog and say "That's Enough" in a pleasant but serious tone, as you pull his head back from your hand.

Romantic (Kisses)

This one is a real delight, unless you hate dog kisses. You can teach this trick quickly by association, simply saying "Kisses" whenever you're getting a licking. To teach your dog to give someone else a kiss, such as the next door neighbor or a member of your audience, use a stick of butter during the teaching phase. Ask a few people to help you out, and rub the backs of their hands with butter before you instruct your dog to give them a kiss. Have them extend their hand to your dog and say "Kisses" as you point to the buttered hand. Soon your dog will be seeking out hands to kiss, butter coated or not!

Loving (Give Me a Hug)

To teach your dog to hug you, kneel down on the floor or sit in a chair. Give the Sit command and check to make sure your dog is sitting square on the floor (not leaning to either side). Next, lift your dog's paws gently and place them on your shoulders as you say "Hug." Give your dog a thorough pet and/or a reward. Then it's "Okay" and help him down. Repeat only three times per session, and stop if your dog is too energetic or starts to nip.

Hand Signals
Cross your arms across your chest.

A hug is just what you need at the end of a long, hard day.

People always ask me if teaching a dog to hug will encourage it to jump. The answer is yes and no. Yes, it encourages jumping if your dog's already started the habit. No, it won't if you have taught your dog the *four paw rule*: a well-mannered dog keeps four on the floor unless they're invited up. If you teach a jumping trick on cue, you can turn it off just as easily. It's the best of both worlds—selective spoiling.

Grrr
Some dogs get too excited standing on two paws. If this is your pal, leave the leash on and give a slight leash correction as you say "Shhh!" Also, try practicing Hug when your dog has less energy.

Polite (Ask Nicely)

Now we're getting onto some more serious maneuvers. This one is a real charmer though, a variation on the old sit up and beg. To teach your dog this trick, I'll need to divide your dogs into three categories: the Naturals, the Corner Crew, and the Bowser Bracers.

The Naturals

These are the dogs who are most inclined to do this trick. They might have even discovered it by themselves during one of their more successful ploys to get attention. If not, you should have no trouble getting them to cooperate.

➤ Instruct Sit and make sure the dog is sitting squarely.

➤ Take a treat and hold it one inch above his nose.

Hand Signals
Move your palm upward, facing the sky.

➤ As he stretches to sniff it, bring it back slowly between his ears as you say "Ask Nicely."

➤ The dog should rise up to follow the path of the treat. Initially click and reward a split-second attempt to sit up. Once he's catching on, hold out for more balanced performances.

The Corner Crew

These eager beavers are often coordinated enough, but are a little too excited about the thought of a biscuit. To structure the learning phase of this trick, follow the steps given previously but start the dog out in a corner of the room. Tuck his back end toward the wall and proceed with training. The walls on either side will help limit and guide his movements.

Sarah Says
If your pal is super excited, practice at a lower energy time such as late in the evening or after a good romp.

Bowser Bracers

If your dog is less than coordinated you might need to be a more active participant in the learning phase.

➤ Sit your dog squarely, instruct "Stay" and position yourself directly behind his tail.

➤ Hold the treat above his nose and bring it upward and back toward his ear.

➤ As you give the command and your dog begins to rise, brace his back with your legs for support.

➤ After initially clicking and rewarding the slightest lift, hold out for more balanced (though still supported) routines.

➤ When your dog can balance well with your help, begin to support him only with your knees.

➤ When he has perfected the trick with knee support, start withdrawing your support incrementally, until you are just standing there cheering your pal on.

Fairly soon you can begin to step away. See how he shines!

Sad (Head Down)

For this one your dog will lie down and place his head or nose between his paws and look up at you with a sad and soulful expression. Of course I'm not suggesting you actually make your dog sad! It's just a trick.

Although they look sad, dogs are actually happy when they're doing tricks for you.

There are two ways to accomplish this maneuver, depending on how active your dog is.

Gentle Hold and Stay

If your dog's a real mush pie, she'll let you manipulate her head gently into position. First get your dog into a Down, and then position her head on the floor between her paws and instruct "Stay." Click if you're using a clicker, reward and praise a three-second stay, slowly increasing the time.

Hand Signals
Clasp your hands together under your chin.

Once your dog can hold herself in this position for ten seconds, start to introduce a word or phrase such as, "Are you *depressed*?" "Are you *sad*?" and have your dog show you by lying down and putting her head between her paws. What a heart stopper!

Lure Lassies

If your dog has no interest in sitting still and truly resists having you manipulate her head, you'll need to be more creative in your approach.

➤ Get your dog into a Down and Stay.

➤ Hold her favorite treat in your thumb, index, and middle fingers so that she can smell it but not eat it.

➤ Lure her head down between her paws using the treat and instruct "Stay." You may have to settle for a nose to the ground at first.

Grrr
When using food as a lure, cage it securely in your fingers and don't release it until *after* you release your dog with "Okay!"

➤ Hold your hand still for three seconds, click, release, and praise. Slowly increase the time until your dog can be still for at least fifteen seconds.

➤ Introduce your catch phrase while you are practicing the trick.

➤ Slowly wean your dog away from your presence on the floor, reward in hand, though you must always reward her for a job well done!

Tired (Go to Sleep)

Growing up, this trick was known as Play Dead. To me the whole dead thing seemed a little depressing; I prefer Go to Sleep—so much more peaceful.

Teaching this trick is not too hard if your dog has mastered the Down and Stay commands.

Hand Signals
Point with your index finger, as if to shoot.

➤ Instruct "Down." Kneel and rub your dog's belly until she's calm.

➤ Gently roll your dog onto her side and command "Stay." If she lifts her head, lovingly rest it back on the floor and command "Stay."

➤ When your dog cooperates, start introducing your trick command, Go to Sleep.

Zany (Chase Your Tail)

A dog chasing his tail is a funny thing to watch, and no one can argue that he's truly mastered the art of having fun with himself. Whether your dog's a natural for this routine or not, it's not a hard one to teach.

Take a biscuit, hold it level with your dog's nose and command "Chase Your Tail" as you *slowly* rotate the treat around his body. I said slowly! Start slow; that's an order!

Reward half spins initially, then full spins, then two, three, four, and so on. Accentuate your hand signal and soon you'll be sending your dog silent cues, no words needed!

Hand Signals
Hold your index finger up and swirl it in a circle.

Sarah Says
This trick is great if you want your dog to wipe his feet. Just command Chase Your Tail while he's standing on a doormat!

Chase Your Tail is a handy command to get your dog to wipe his feet.

Sneezy

There are several reasons why you might want to teach your dog to sneeze on cue. First of all, what better way to bond than with a healthy sneeze-off between you two? And the next time you have guests over, you can ask your dog, "Who's your favorite dwarf?"

➤ Go to your dog and tell her to Sit.

➤ Blow into her nose gently from about a distance of two or three feet.

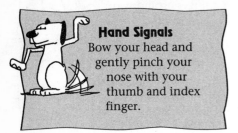

Hand Signals
Bow your head and gently pinch your nose with your thumb and index finger.

➤ This should encourage her to sneeze. When she does, pinch your nose with two fingers and say "Ahh-Choo!"

➤ If you're a theatrical sort you'll be able to get your dog to sneeze with you for the fun of it. A sneeze-off!

➤ Soon try to get her to sneeze, hand signal only!

Embarrassed (Hide Your Face)

I've saved my toughest mood for last. But oh, how endearing to see your dog hide her face behind her paw. You'll teach this trick so that your dog will respond to a hand signal only, and you can lead up to it with questions like "How do you feel when I catch you on the counter?" or "Would you like some beans with your dinner?" or "I heard you met a fancy Poodle the other day...."

Getting your dog to do this one is a real art form. First you must get her in a calm, cooperative mood. If she's got too much energy, she'll quickly get frustrated and quit. Next you must practice your Paw command. Now you're ready to begin.

➤ Take your dog into a quiet area and tell her "Sit."

➤ Practice a few Paw commands.

➤ Hold a treat down low and on the opposite side of the paw your dog has been giving you. In other words, if your dog has been giving you her right paw, hold the treat to her left side.

➤ You may need to gently hold the skin below her neck to brace her head into position as her paw comes up.

➤ When her paw and nose meet, mark the moment with a clicker or a "Yes!" and reward and praise.

➤ Stop after she makes three contacts, rewarding the session generously with a favorite game.

➤ Do not practice more than four sessions a day.

If your dog is clueless with the above procedure, you'll need to get more ingenious with your training techniques. This is what I call the induced training method.

➤ Take your dog into a quiet area and instruct "Sit."

➤ Have on hand your treat rewards and your clicker.

➤ Stick a little loop of cellophane tape *lightly* to the side of your dog's nose.

➤ When he lifts his paw to knock it off, click, reward, and praise.

➤ When your dog catches on to the game, start to introduce a command such as Hide Your Face and blatantly scratch the side of your nose as a hand signal.

Hand Signals
Cuff the side of your nose.

Grrr
Only use cellophane tape, and only stick it on lightly. You don't want to hurt your dog by pulling out his hair along with the tape.

➤ Initially reward your dog regardless of the position she gets into to remove the tape from her nose. Gradually shape the behavior to what you're looking for.

Now you're ready for show time. Practice this one in more and more distracting areas before inviting an audience to witness your brilliant pal at work.

Mix and Match

Be creative when teaching your dog these tricks. If you can tie in a unique hand signal your dog will not only learn to watch you better, but will perform happily with no words needed.

Now you can really start having some fun! For example, after you ask your dog for his favorite dwarf and he sneezes, follow up with his least favorite dwarf and give the Go to Sleep command.

Sarah Says
When practicing difficult tricks, use the KISS theory: Keep It Short and Sweet.

The Least You Need to Know

➤ Getting your dog to display moods, from happy to sad to everything in between, is a real crowd pleaser. And dogs really love the attention. Ham it up with your dog and remember, it's all in the name of fun!

➤ When teaching your dog tricks, always start with easy ones. When you're teaching the more difficult moods, finish your practice session with your dog's favorite mood (such as happy or romantic) to make sure you're ending on a positive note.

➤ Some routines can be taught in several ways, depending on the temperament of your dog. Read each of the options before you start practicing with your dog.

➤ If you can think of a better way to communicate your wishes to your dog, try it! If it works, write to me and I'll see if I can get it into the next printing of this book.

Chapter 9

Everyday Miracles

In This Chapter

➤ Teaching your dog to potty in one designated place

➤ Settling down for a rest

➤ Picking up, doggy style

➤ Closing cupboards, Say Your Prayers, and more

This chapter is about manners. While every dog should have the basic good manners to sit, stay, not jump, and not pull, you can invite a *really* mannerly dog to dinner and it will know exactly which fork to use. In fact, these tricks are so mannerly and endearing that you can take your dog to dinner with the Queen.

Potty in One Place

No small miracle! And your dog must be fully housebroken before you attempt this little trick. This is what I want you to do:

➤ Select a sacred Bathroom Area in your yard.

➤ Take your dog to the specific spot, first thing in the morning. When she goes, praise and treat (the clicker is optional).

➤ Find some thick white clothesline and lay it out in a six-foot circle around your dog's elimination.

Grrr
Do not leave more than one elimination in the circle, and as soon as your dog learns this trick, pick up *everything* promptly. No dog will go where she's gone twenty times before. Would you?

➤ Next time you take your dog out to potty, go to this area and ignore your dog.

➤ If your dog goes potty in the circle, click and treat. If not, praise calmly but no treat.

If your dog decides to play with the rope, soak it overnight in Bitter Apple Spray (found in local pet supply stores), a nontoxic substance with a taste dogs find unpleasant. Have faith! Soon your dog will be as potty trained as a six-year-old.

City Canines

So you don't have a three-acre spread in the country. Don't feel bad. The circle trick can work for you too; you'll just need to shrink your circumference and curb it: *That's the law!* Your dog may even need to adjust to a shape other than a circle, but the plan is similar; reward deposits made inside the rope, lightly praise those done outside.

Paper Plans

Got an indoor dog? The circle trick may not be necessary, as your dog will usually go wherever the paper is placed. If you're a seasoned traveler, however, a portable rope outlining the paper can help ease the travel transition for your dog.

Settle in One Spot

This is one of those lessons you appreciate for the rest of your life. Pick an area for your dog in each room. I advise a spot that is to the side or in a quiet corner; in my other books I refer to it as a station. Adorn your dog's station with a toy and bedding, if that's what she likes.

Each time you are in the room and you'd like your dog to quiet down, instruct her to Settle Down as you point to her area. If she ignores you, lead her there and say "Settle" as you position her in a comfortable Down and instruct "Stay." If your dog challenges her

Stay command, secure a leash to an immovable object near the station, leaving just enough slack for your dog to lie down comfortably.

Soon you'll be able to point and your dog will go happily, content to chew her favorite toy and stay out from under foot. If you'd like to create a permanent doggy spot in the TV room or the bedroom, consider placing it near your couch or bed. Dogs love being close!

Sarah Says
Betcha haven't thought of this one! If you've got small kids, or if your dog's still a pup, attach your dog's toy to a piece of rope and tie it to something immovable near the station spot. That way it won't disappear.

Tell Me You're Hungry

Growing up, I had a Collie named Meghan who was my pride and joy. I remember saving every dollar I had until there was enough to buy her. One of her most endearing qualities was to bring me gifts. If I was happy, she'd always bring over a ball to play. If I had a bad day, I could always count on Meghan greeting me at the bus with a leaf or twig or some other earthly treasure. And heaven forbid I was two minutes late to feed her; she would always drop her food dish in my lap.

How do you teach your dog this charming little trick? You need to start out with a dog that is comfortable putting things in her mouth. If your dog won't pick up anything short of a biscuit, then she might not be the best candidate.

Are you still with me? Let's proceed:

➤ Take your dog aside with treats and her food dish. If you're using a stainless steel bowl (which I recommend), tie a cotton cloth around the rim.

➤ Ask your dog, "Are you hungry?" and wave the bowl in front of her face. When she clamps on, praise, click, and treat.

➤ Practice until your dog makes the connection that grasping the bowl is the name of the game.

➤ Now hold the bowl closer to the floor. Lift the bowl an inch from the floor and swish it back and forth as you ask, "Are you hungry?" When the dog takes the bowl, click if you're using a clicker, and reward.

➤ Drum roll please! Place the bowl on the floor, stand up straight and ask, "Are you hungry?" Praise any interest your dog shows in the bowl. Reward any contact.

Grrr
Do not play this game at feeding time or with your dog's bowl full of food. You do *not* want to teach her to snatch her food bowl from your hand.

➤ As the light flashes in your dog's head, begin to ask the dog to Come, and gently take the bowl from her mouth. Eventually, reward only deliveries.

Pick Up Your Toys

Always shopping for your dog? Well don't feel bad; I'm a bit of a toy freak myself. My favorites are the animal toys that sound like the animals themselves: a cow that moos, a frog that ribbets, a pig that oinks. Guess I'm easily amused.

Bet You Didn't Know

Do you have both kids and dog? Here's a good project. Have the kids decorate a toy box for their dog. Let their creative juices run rampant: magazine cut-outs, photos, drawings, computer print-outs; no limits. Your dog will love it in any case.

If your house has begun to look like a mine field, you might want to teach your dog Tidy Up!

➤ First you'll need a toy box, and a designated area set aside for it. It's a big decision; you can't change its location for a while.

➤ Bring your dog to his box with a favorite toy.

➤ Give him the toy.

➤ Snap your fingers over the box. When your dog leans his head over the box, tell him "Drop-Tidy Up," click, and offer a treat (which should encourage your dog to drop the toy).

➤ Repeat this four times.

➤ Stop and remove the box.

➤ Repeat these sessions once or twice a day.

Hand Signals
Sweep the room with an outstretched finger.

➤ As your dog catches on, try giving him the toy farther and farther from his box (which should always be in the same area).

➤ After he catches on to this step, go near the box again, but this time leave the toy on the floor and encourage your dog to pick it up.

➤ Now try for two toys. Start by only rewarding a two-toy drop. Then a three-toy drop, then four.

Now you're ready to start hiring out your very own four-footed maid service!

Open and Shut

Teaching your dog to open and shut the cupboards is one clever act, but it's two separate skills, and you have to teach them one by one.

Shutting Doors

This trick requires the Touch command (remember it from Chapter 3?). Review it if necessary. It's best to use a clicker or some other device.

➤ Hold out a greeting card or an index card to your dog and say "Touch." Click, treat, and praise.

➤ Move around the room, holding the card in various locations, giving the Touch command. Don't move on to the next step until your dog has got this one down pat.

➤ Drum roll please. Tape the card to a cupboard door and open the door slightly. Tape the card at your dog's chin level. Nothing too high; nothing too low.

➤ Command "Touch," and reward the slightest effort, even if your dog doesn't shut the cupboard completely.

➤ As your dog catches on, open the door and command "Shut It" as you point to the cupboard door. Reward only those touches that snap the cupboard tightly closed.

Hand Signals
Point to the intended door or cupboard.

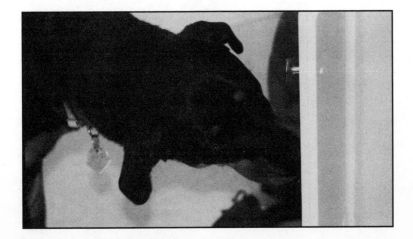

Teaching your dog to shut the cupboard door is just a variation of that old trick, Touch.

Now you're ready to expand to other doors in the house. Remember to start each new adventure with the door only slightly open, and progress slowly.

Opening Doors

When teaching this command I usually divide dogs into two categories: paw or mouth expressive. Either way, you'll need to make a rope handle and attach it to the door at either paw or mouth height.

Mouth Expressive   First, wiggle the rope and pique your dog's interest away from the door. When your dog starts mouthing the rope, attach it to the door handle and reward your dog for pulling it on location.

Paw Expressive   Attach the rope to the door handle, pretend to paw at it, and reward your dog for copying you. Once you've piqued your dog's interest, follow this series of steps:

➤ Reward each contact with the rope, then;

➤ Reward only those contacts that open the door slightly, then;

➤ Reward only those contacts that fully open the door.

Now you've got a dog who can not only open the cupboard to take what she wants, but who can cover her tracks by closing it!

Get Your Leash

It's a true fact of nature that dogs love to go for walks. To teach them this little trick might be inviting some late night leash deliveries, but you decide. I think bringing their leash is pretty ingenious, and it's a simple trick to master. Here we go!

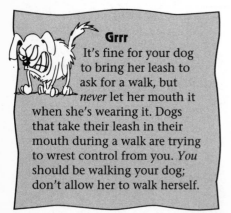

Grrr
It's fine for your dog to bring her leash to ask for a walk, but *never* let her mouth it when she's wearing it. Dogs that take their leash in their mouth during a walk are trying to wrest control from you. *You* should be walking your dog; don't allow her to walk herself.

➤ When your dog is not wearing her leash, encourage her to take it in her mouth.

➤ When she'll do it readily, say "Get Your Leash!" and click and treat.

➤ Fold the leash neatly and secure it with a rubber band or string. Place it on the couch and encourage your dog to get it by saying "Get Your Leash!" and pointing to it.

➤ If your dog grabs it, click and treat (even for only a partial return).

➤ Repeat the preceding step, but only reward when your dog brings the leash to you.

➤ Remove the string and let your dog drag the leash to you. Its weight and pull may seem awkward at first, but praise your dog as you encourage her to come to you.

➤ Go to the area where you keep the leash and place it in an obvious spot. Stand just a few feet away and encourage your dog's delivery.

➤ Extend your distance from the leash as you repeat the request, and reward good deliveries.

Say Your Prayers

This is a dear little trick. The goal is to have your dog place her paws on any object and lower her head reverently. Are you laughing? I'm serious!

This big girl knows how to say her prayers!

➤ Sit your dog squarely in front of you and show her a treat. You should sit, too.

➤ Lift her paws gently onto your lap.

➤ Hold the treat in between her paws and under your legs, so she has to drop her head between her paws to reach for it. Tell her to Stay as you let her lick the treat. Say "Okay" as you give her the treat, and praise her.

➤ After she catches on to this sequence and can hold her head still for ten seconds, begin to use the phrase "Say Your Prayers."

➤ Now practice telling her to rest her paws on other things, such as a bed or chair. Offer the treat over the back of a chair, for instance, always using Say Your Prayers.

The Least You Need to Know

➤ Having a dog that will eliminate in a designated place is a real advantage. No yellow stains marking up the lawn, no standing outside for hours waiting for your dog to go, a handy travel cue to take with you on trips; the benefits are endless!

➤ Most tricks are taught bit by bit. Make sure your dog has mastered one part of the trick before you move on to the next.

➤ Praise even small movements in the right direction, and give them a command when they occur. Pretty soon your dog will be acting on cue for you.

Leap Dog

In This Chapter

➤ Teach your dog to jump over, through, and into all kinds of objects (including you)

➤ How to find the optimum jumping height for your dog's size

➤ Discouraging inappropriate jumping

It's no secret, dogs love to jump: on guests, counters, family members, each other—it's all one big game. But for those of you who are less than delighted at your dog's enthusiasm for standing on two paws, read closely. The best way to teach your dog when not to jump is to teach her when she can jump. Redirect that enthusiasm, and put it on cue. Here's how.

Over

Structured jumping must start somewhere, so here we go. Get a broom or a straight pole. In a carpeted area, balance the pole on two objects of equal height. Make sure it's secure enough so that it can't be easily knocked over.

How high should the pole be? To start, measure the height between your dog's paw and his shoulder. Divide this in half, then subtract an inch. That's how high your training jump should be. (Later, when your dog learns this trick, you can make it higher.)

The training jump for this dog should be 11 inches.

24 inches ÷ 2 = 12 inches

12 inches − 1 =11 inches

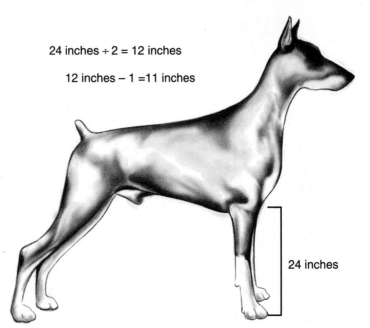

24 inches

Bet You Didn't Know

How are dogs and airplanes similar? They both need runways. To make sure your dog has enough runway, clear space for five strides coming up to the jump and four once she's cleared it. Zoom!

Now you're ready to begin. Place your dog on a short leash for control.

➤ Let your dog sniff the jump. Discourage any test chewing with a light "Ep, ep."

➤ Bring your dog back and say "Over" before you move toward the jump.

➤ Jog up lightly and jump just ahead of your dog.

➤ If your dog refuses, stay calm. Walk over the jump several times while your dog watches, then try to walk over it together. It may take a few goes, but your dog will soon overcome her fears.

➤ Now, pick up the pace. Move at your dog's natural gait, not too fast and not too slow.

➤ Once your dog takes the jump with pride, stop just before the jump and let your dog do it alone. Reward with a jackpot of treats and praise.

➤ Stop your approach further and further back from the jump. Say "Over" before you send your dog, pointing to the intended obstacle.

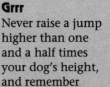

Hand Signals
Sweep your arm toward the jump.

When you're still teaching this trick, walk over the jump right behind your dog and praise her before she has a chance to turn back and retrace her path back to you.

Grrr
Never raise a jump higher than one and a half times your dog's height, and remember many dogs will only be comfortable jumping at lower heights.

Once your dog learns how to jump properly, you can raise the jump to a height appropriate to your dog. Set up an obstacle course, directing your dog to each jump with a sweep of your arm. Set up jumps in your driveway, yard, or a nearby park. Practice your Over command when you come across a natural obstacle, such as a railing or a fallen branch.

Over the Kids

Kids also make good natural obstacles (as any parent will tell you). And while kids don't exactly get into the Sit, Stay, and Come exercises, they do like to join in fun tricks with their dog.

For this trick, have the kids and the dog practice Over with the broom so the dog gets used to performing around the children first. The next step will depend on how many kids you've got.

One Kid. Ask your child to lie down under or alongside the jump. Take your dog and let her sniff the new setup. Say "Ep, ep" if she gets excited and lead her back five strides. Say "Over," run toward the jump, and leap together. Send your dog alone once she cooperates.

Slowly encourage your child to raise her back toward the ceiling until you find the right height for your dog. When your child has friends visiting you can add another child.

More Than One Kid. Always start the kid jump with one child, as described previously. If you want to add children, first let the dog jump over them one at a time, just to get used to each child. Then begin to line the kids out flat, on either side of the broom jump.

One at a time they should raise their backs to a height that's comfortable for your dog. Be realistic though: Don't add so many kids that your dog is forced to step over them like rocks across a stream.

Through

Jumping through something is a natural progression from Over and really adds zing to any trick routine (make sure your dog really is comfortable with Over before you try Through). Your dog can jump through a hoop, into your arms, or through a car window.

The Hoop

Let's start with the hoop. Go out to your local variety store and dig a hula hoop out of the corner. Though its place on the shelf has been taken by electronic pastimes, you can still find a hula hoop if you look hard enough.

Set up your original jumping pole across a threshold or between two pieces of furniture. Put your dog on a short lead, and let her sniff the hoop as you position it on the floor in the center of the jump. Ask someone to hold the hoop or prop it up securely. Instruct your dog "Over" as you run toward the obstacle, letting go of the hand lead as you get close.

After your dog cooperates, start adding the command Through to Over as you start for the jump, like this: "Over-Through."

Sarah Says
If your dog refuses the hoop, let her watch as you climb in and out cheerfully. Standing on one side, toss a cherished treat through to the other side and lead your dog through calmly.

Next, hold or prop the hoop higher so it is even with the height of the pole. Now your dog might hesitate because the hoop looks, well, like a hoop, not like a level jump. If this is the case, approach it slowly and let your dog walk through it a couple of times, using food to encourage her.

Now you're ready to try the hoop alone. Using another threshold or restricted area, prop or hold the hoop securely on the floor. Instructing "Through," trot up to the jump and let your dog go through alone. Praise her joyously and encourage her to go back through by running backward yourself. Clap, sing, praise, treat—let your dog know what a star she is!

Progressively raise the hoop to a height appropriate for your dog. Once she's comfortable with this routine in a restricted area, start working her in more open areas. Keep your praise and energy high; this display's a real crowd pleaser.

This is a lot more fun than trying to wiggle this hoop around your waist.

Your Arms

If you have a small to medium dog, this trick is a heart warmer. If you're truly daring you can try it with a large dog, but let me warn you: Watch out for your nose. One of my brightest students, a chipper Chocolate Lab, had mastered every trick I knew, so I decided to give this trick a try. Of course, once he figured out what I wanted he was eager to give it his all. Unfortunately, one day my nose got in the way and there was blood everywhere. Poor boy—he thought he'd killed me.

➤ Approach this trick as with the hoop, placing your arms in a hoop shape with one elbow on the floor.

➤ It's easier to have an extra person around to lure your dog through your arms with a treat as you say "Through." But if you want to try it solo, place your dog in a Stay on one side of a doorway, show him a treat, toss it to the other side of the doorway and release with "Okay-Through" as you position your arms.

➤ Your praise must be ecstatic and uplifting. What a great dog you have!

➤ Progressively hold your arms higher and slowly work out of the restrictions of the doorway.

A Car Window

Have you got an athletic type dog? My dear Husky Kyia would run to the car and jump into the window with a hand signal alone. This wowed everyone and really highlighted her car trips, though my car did get a wee bit scratched. If you can live with a few scratches, here's how to teach it:

➤ Place your dog in a Sit-Stay fifteen feet from the car.

➤ Open the door of the car and toss in your dog's favorite toy.

➤ Enthusiastically command "Go to the Car" and point to the open spot.

➤ Reward warmly and repeat this three times at each lesson for three days.

➤ Next, open your car window (make sure you use a window that rolls down fully). With your dog at your heel, show her the opening, letting her place two paws on the car door.

➤ Toss in her toy as she watches, then lead her back fifteen paces.

➤ Run with her to the car as you point, saying "Go to the Car." If she doesn't jump in, reassure her and encourage her to rest her paws on the door.

➤ Though you may have to ease her hind end into the car, soon your dog will look forward to hearing "Go to the Car" whenever you say it.

Grrr

Kyia did two things with this trick I want to warn you about. Once, when we were walking, a woman in a car stopped us to ask directions. Kyia, sensing her distressed tone, jumped in her window to lift her spirits. On a more serious note, one day I sent her to the car, only to learn someone had shut the window. Kyia was okay, but never send your dog to a closed window.

Fire Rings

If you're clever enough to accomplish this trick, join the circus. As my Mama told me, never play with fire.

Into

Dogs, being dogs, love to jump into things. In fact, sometimes the real trick is getting them to jump out. (More on that later.) The hardest decision for me was where to start this section.

Your Lap

Dogs love laps. Getting them to jump there, however, is a stunt that is somewhat restricted by size. Avoid this trick if your dog weighs more than you, or weighs under five pounds. Small dogs have big hearts but short legs; don't push them.

➤ Put your dog in a Stay across the room. Show your dog his favorite toy or treat.

➤ Sit in a low chair. Patting your lap say "Name" and "Come," then "Up."

➤ The first time you try this, the dog may run over and stop short or put two paws up. Praise and offer a treat anyway, and lead him back to the starting point. Reward any attempts to join you the first three tries.

➤ Eventually, reward only for landing in your lap.

Is your dog earthbound in disbelief? The next time she approaches, gently grasp her collar under her chin and ease her up. Reward that. Soon she'll be leaping at your invitation.

Hand Signals
Pat your lap.

A Chair

Are those sad hound dog eyes melting your heart while you're trying to eat? Among my many options for handling dogs and dining, let me add this one to the list: a formal invitation.

➤ Attach a piece of carpet or toweling to a dining chair (for better footing).

➤ Encourage your dog onto the chair by saying something funny, such as "Dinner Time," as you pat the chair and help your dog onto the seat.

➤ Because dogs like to be up, you should have no problem convincing your dog that this is the place to be, but now you'll need her to sit still while you push in her chair. Try using the Stay command, moving the chair in little by little.

Of course, now that your dog is sitting at the dinner table, it's your job to figure out what to do with her.

Up Into Your Arms

One of my favorite pals is named Buddy, a large-boned Yorkshire Terrier and a champion-into-your-arms jumper. Open your arms and call to him and he'll be up giving you a kiss before you can blink your eyes.

Hand Signals
Bend your knees and pat your thighs.

*Buddy is on his
way up for a kiss.*

To get your dog to do this trick, start out kneeling in front of her, encouraging her up to your face with your arms extended. She'll probably use your body like a ladder; be prepared. Next, leave your dog in a Stay across the room while you continue to kneel in a low position. Call her with "Come, Up!" Praise like mad when she ends up in your arms.

After your dog catches on to the run and jump, begin to rise slowly. Soon your dog will jump into your arms for the sheer delight of a kiss.

When Not to Jump

Everybody knows a jumper, a knock-you-over-when-you-come-in jumper, a muddy-paw-prints-on-the-couch jumper, a counter cruiser. So what can you do? The first step in solving your problem is to remember the chief motivation for your dog's jumping: attention. Jumping is a sure-fire attention getter. Your dog will die for it. And if she jumps up and you yell at her, it's attention nonetheless. That makes jumping a guaranteed rewarding activity. So why should she stop?

The first step in resolving any jumping problem is to remove the reward and let your dog do the math herself. Here are some solutions to the most typical situations. If you're still frustrated with this problem, take a look at *The Complete Idiot's Guide to Choosing, Training, and Raising a Dog* (also by me!) for more in-depth solutions.

There are definitely times when it's a bad idea to jump on the couch.

Homecoming

You have two choices 'when you come home: Either ignore your dog, crossing your arms and looking up (encouraging everyone in the house to do the same); or you can use Binaca Mouth Spray (which can be ordered using the form in the back of the book) to create an invisible boundary between you and your dog. If you choose to spray, make sure you do not look into your dog's eyes and don't ever spray your dog directly. Create an invisible boundary by spraying a space between yourself and your dog. (Your dog may get sprayed on the nose if she disregards the boundary and that's okay; just don't aim for your dog or look at her.)

> **Sarah Says**
> Have a basket of balls or a squeak toy by the door and toss one down when you come in. This teaches your dog to focus her energy on her toy, not you.

Company

After your dog catches on to the Binaca Mouth Spray correction, you can use it to keep her away from company. Using the same principles of an invisible boundary and no attention, you can discourage your dog's two-pawed greeting without making a fuss. Toss a toy on the ground to encourage better methods of releasing excitement. And make sure your guests know not to greet the dog until she's settled down.

Bet You Didn't Know

Dogs mimic your energy level. If you come home to an excited dog, or if your dog flips out when the doorbell rings, stay calm. If you get excited in your attempts to calm your dog, you'll actually be getting your dog supercharged.

Counter Cruisers

Do you have one of these? A dog that cruises the kitchen counter for crumbs, or sneaks a paw to steal a tidbit. It's a nasty little habit that's hard to break.

First of all, realize that once your dog is on the counter or has successfully stolen a bite, you cannot correct her. Let it go. Any corrections after the fact will come across as Prize Envy (your dog thinking that because you're interested in what she's doing or what's she's stolen, that the object must be truly valuable).

To discourage a counter cruiser, you'll need to correct the thought process. Each time you see your dog sniffing the counter, say "Don't Think About It!" in a no-nonsense tone. Because you're smarter than her, you might try setting up situations (say, a piece of pizza on the kitchen counter) where you can catch your dog contemplating a theft and administer the correction.

To correct a counter cruiser, you have to catch her in the act.

The Furniture Fan Club

Most people invite their puppies on the furniture, only to regret it later. To discourage your dog from getting onto the furniture, attach a short lead to his buckle collar and pull him off each time he puts even one paw on the furniture, saying "Excuse Me!" in a very lofty tone.

Sarah Says
If you're still having trouble with this habit, check out one of my other training books for a lengthier explanation.

The Least You Need to Know

➤ Dogs love jumping. If you don't redirect their impulses, you'll live to regret it.

➤ Jumping tricks are fun to teach, especially for children. Disguised in every routine are more formal commands such as Stay and Come.

➤ After your dog knows the basic Over command, you can extend it to more exciting tricks like Through the Hoop and Into My Arms.

➤ Never ask your dog to jump higher than he's physically able.

Noisy Tricks

In This Chapter

➤ Teaching your dog to bark on cue

➤ Teaching your dog not to bark on cue

➤ Sounding the alarm, singing, counting, and more

➤ Redeeming the problem barker

Does your dog love to make noise? Does he bark when he's happy, excited, when he doesn't get his way? Is your biggest question not how to train him to be vocal, but how to shut it off? Actually, it's easier than you think. You start by training him to do something he already likes to do: bark! Then you can turn him on and off.

Once you have a greater appreciation for your dog's natural vocal talents, you'll need to do a little coaching. Are you ready Maestro?

Ready on Four

To teach your dog to bark on command, you'll need to use eye contact, hand signals, and voice commands.

Eye Contact Look at your dog alertly when you want him to bark. Break your stare when you want him to quiet down.

Voice Command You'll need two—Speak and Shhh. Enunciate clearly when you give your commands.

Hand Signals
You need a snappy hand signal for Speak; try snapping your fingers near your mouth. For Shhh, put your index finger to your lips as if you were shushing a baby.

Lesson One. Get something your dog lives for; a ball or treat for example. Secure him to a post or tree and hold his prized object just out of reach while you encourage "Speak" and look at him intensely. When he does bark, reward him cheerfully. Begin to add the hand signal to your voice and eye cues. Repeat this procedure until your dog reacts quickly to the Speak command.

Lesson Two. Encourage your dog to speak throughout the day for positive things, such as a meal or a walk. If he speaks out of turn, just ignore him.

Lesson Three. Now it's time to turn your dog's focus to Shhh. Go back to Lesson One, securing him and standing in front of him with something tasty or fun. Say "Speak!" After a few barks say "Shhh," stamp your foot and avert your eyes. Click if you're using a clicker, reward, and praise. Repeat this process until your dog responds to both Speak and Shhh.

Lesson Four. Practice your commands throughout the day, varying which ones you reinforce. Sometimes reward the Speak, sometimes the Shhh. Have your dog Speak and Shhh two or three times before rewarding him. He'll be so proud of his new trick, and so will you!

Alarm Dog

Believe it or not, some dogs don't bark when the doorbell rings. But even if yours does, teaching her to bark on cue will also help her stop barking (there's more on problem barkers at the end of this chapter). To help your dog learn to bark when the doorbell rings, ring it yourself.

➤ Put your dog on a Sit-Stay and stand at the open door.

➤ Ring the bell and command "Speak"; click and reward the inevitable bark.

➤ Ring the bell again, instruct "Speak," but wait until your dog responds to "Shhh" before you reward her.

➤ Now ask a neighbor to come by and ring the bell or knock when your dog is not expecting company. Reinforce Speak or Shhh—whichever happens to be your dog's weak suit.

➤ Repeat the process in your car. While the car is parked in the driveway, have someone approach, telling your dog to bark on cue. As your dog learns this one, you can gradually work up to parking lots and even gas stations.

Sarah Says
After your dog learns Speak, Bark to Go Out is a really simple variation. Start first thing in the morning when your dog really has to go. Go to the door, tell her "Speak," and don't open the door until she does. What's the secret password?

Fire Alarm

Some dogs naturally don't like fire. This is rather intelligent, when you think about it. My dog while growing up, a Shepherd mix named Shawnee, hated fire, especially a burning cigarette. She was a quiet soul and would disappear whenever anyone lit up. These days, though, it's not such a bad thing to teach your dog to speak up whenever someone lights up.

Once your dog knows how to bark at a lit match, she'll also be your fire alarm.

➤ Gather a book of matches, treats, a clicker if you use one, and a toy for good measure.

➤ Put your dog on a Sit-Stay and light a match.

➤ When the flame rises say "Put It Out" and give your hand signal and eye contact for Speak.

➤ Blow the flame out when your dog barks; click and reward as usual.

➤ Repeat and repeat, increasing your focus on a quick response. Now you have a built-in fire alarm!

Singing the Blues

Some dogs just sing the blues naturally. The arctic breeds, shepherds, and hound dogs are notorious for letting a out howl when they hear music or get excited. Others you can teach to sing.

Monkey see, monkey do applies here. Play some soulful music and let out a good howl yourself. Toss your head back and hit the high notes! Whether your dog joins in this session or the next, let yourself go and end by playing your dog's favorite game. Soon his tail will beat the floor whenever you pass by the stereo.

When your dog joins in, congratulate him and keep on howling. To signal a howl, lean your head back, face to the moon, and purse those lips. Now you can think of clever questions to ask your dog. What does a werewolf do when he sees a full moon? What do you say when you see your girlfriend/boyfriend? Clever dog!

Singing the blues is a natural for the arctic breeds.

Counting and Other Complex Math Problems

This is where your bark-training efforts really pay off. People will be thrilled to see your dog doing better in math than they did in high school.

Before you start asking your dog to count anything, you must polish his Speak and Shhh skills, so he can do them with hand signals alone (if you give the voice commands, some doubters may believe it's not really your dog who's counting). Once you've got the commands down pat, you can begin asking your dog some basic questions. Just give the Speak hand signal, count the barks, and then signal Shhh. Try these to start:

➤ How much is two plus two?

➤ How old are you?

➤ How many eggs in a half dozen?

Work on your silent communication, so that no one can tell you're helping out. Once your dog can answer the basics, you can proceed to more difficult math problems:

➤ How many stars in the Big Dipper? (The answer is seven.)

➤ What's the square root of sixty-four? (You should know this one!)

➤ If two sides of a right triangle are each two inches long, how many inches long is the third side? (Three, of course—let your dog round off the decimal.)

The Bothersome Barker

A barking dog is a real headache. How you handle your situation will depend on what is prompting your dog to bark in the first place. But whatever you do, don't yell—yelling is barking in Doglish, and instead of calming your dog it will rile him up. To solve your problem, stay cool. Let's break up the barkers into categories.

At the Door

Most everyone appreciates a dog alarm at the door; a few woofs to announce new arrivals. It gets annoying, however, when the alarm can't be shut off. After all, enough is enough. The ideal situation is to have an alarm bark with an off switch. Here's how:

➤ Place a penny can or breath spray and a clicker or treat cup at the door.

Sarah Says
To make a penny can, fill an empty soda can with ten pennies and tape the top. The shaking sound startles dogs.

➤ Position someone outside the door and ask them to ring the bell ten times every twenty seconds.

Grrr
Never hold your dog back while you open the door. It's like holding a frantic child; it will only make him more wild. Also, approach the door calmly. Running to the door and screaming at your dog will create a frenzy.

➤ When your dog starts barking say "Speak" and approach the door calmly. Praise him and then say "Shhh."

➤ If needed, support your command with a shake of the penny can or a squirt in front of his nose. (You may even need to let your dog drag a hand leash to snap a little sense into him!) Click, treat, and praise your dog when he quiets down.

➤ Repeat and repeat until your dog gets the hang of it. Now try it with a real guest.

Motion Detector

Got one of those dogs who barks at everything she sees and hears? This type of barking can be really rewarding for your dog, because whenever she barks at something, whether from the window or the yard, it goes away. Sure, you and I know that the postman and the kids on their way to school are going to keep moving anyway, but your dog doesn't know that.

How do you remedy your motion detector?

➤ Avoid leaving your dog alone outdoors for long stretches of time. Confinement often breeds boredom and territorial behavior. Put those two together and you're likely to end up with a barkaholic.

➤ Don't yell; screaming is barking in Doglish. Your dog will feel supported, not discouraged.

➤ Any time you see (or hear) your dog start to perk up, say "Shhh" and use your clicker or treat cup to encourage her to come. If your dog ignores you, leave a hand lead on her collar and use it for reinforcement. If necessary, use a spritzer or penny can to help break your dog's focus.

➤ If your fellow is a night watchman, you'll need to station him in your room. Give him a bed, a bone, and secure his lead to something stationary. Bed time!

➤ Last but not least, give your dog an outlet for barking by teaching the noisy tricks outlined in this chapter.

Bet You Didn't Know

Dogs who bark at everything perceive themselves as your leader. One of the leader's duties is to guard their territory and pack from intruders. All the other training and interaction you're doing will help your dog focus on and respect you as the leader of the pack. That's important; without that, you'll be hard pressed to make any impression.

Car Trouble

Being locked in a car with a barking dog is my version of purgatory. The car creates a territorial situation similar to the one described previously. Your dog barks, and whatever is outside disappears. In the case of a moving car, it disappears even faster! Yelling at your dog isn't the thing to do. Pleading won't help either. This problem needs a good training regime. Here are some things to get you started:

➤ Instruct "Wait" before you let your dog enter or exit the car and give permission with "Okay." It's your car, your territory; don't let him forget that.

➤ Enforce stillness while you drive. Station your dog in the car with a Seat Belt Safety Lead (you can order one using the form in the back of the book) or another car safety device.

➤ Ignore the barking if your car is moving. Driving is a job all by itself.

➤ If you're stationary, spritz your dog with breath spray or a shake penny can and say "Shhh."

➤ Whenever your dog is quiet, reward him with your clicker and/or treats.

➤ If your dog barks at attendants, ask them to toss a piece of cheese into the car window from afar. The idea is to give your dog a more positive association with people who approach the car.

Sarah Says
If your dog enjoys the scent of breath spray, try a spray bottle filled half with vinegar and half with water instead.

Attention Hound

Imagine this: You're sitting reading the Sunday paper when suddenly your dog comes out of nowhere and starts barking for a pat. Cute, huh? Not really. So what should you do?

Giving in would make you look like a servant. Yelling would be counter-productive. Got any ideas? Here are two:

➤ Occasionally, turn to your dog and instruct "Speak!" Let him bark a couple of times, then say "Shhh" and ignore him. Walk away if you need to, but don't give in and pay attention.

➤ When your dog is barking for attention, that's the time to ignore her. Otherwise you're teaching her that barking is a very effective tool. I know, it may give you a headache, but let me suggest wax ear plugs. They work wonders.

Protest Barking

Some dogs don't like to be left alone. To tell you the truth, neither do I. If you return and soothe a protest barker, you'll end up with a really spoiled dog on your hands—one who has trained you.

On the other hand, if you ignore the protest barking, your neighbors, or even your spouse may protest. Is there a happy medium? Not really, but I'll give you some suggestions.

➤ Ignore it if you can. Never yell.

➤ Avoid grand departures and arrivals; they're too stimulating.

➤ Dogs like to be with you. When you're home, let them.

➤ Place peanut butter in a hollow rubber bone and give it to your dog as you leave. It's a tasty way to keep him busy!

➤ Return to your dog only after he's calmed down. If you must interfere with his barking tantrum, go quietly without eye contact or comments, place him on the Teaching Lead tied around your waist and ignore him for half an hour while you lead him around.

Still Having Problems?

If you've got a truly problem dog, flip through *The Complete Idiot's Guide for Choosing, Training, and Raising a Dog* for more detailed instructions. And until you can get to the bookstore, remember:

➤ Never yell at a barking dog.

➤ Make sure you're in front of your dog before a Shhh command. If you're behind him you're the back-up barker.

➤ Don't focus on your dog or make prolonged eye contact when giving a correction. Eye contact actually reinforces behavior.

➤ After your dog quiets down, click, reward, and refocus his attention with a game.

The Least You Need to Know

➤ Barking tricks are great for dogs that love to make noise.

➤ You'll need to teach your dog verbal and visual cues to start and stop barking. Be patient and invest in some ear plugs.

➤ Teaching a dog to bark is the first step in teaching a dog not to bark. The next step is understanding why your dog barks, and addressing the underlying problem.

The K-9 Express

Having a retriever in your home has many perks: the fun of fetch, a helper to carry in the groceries, slippers delivered to your chilly feet. There are few things as astounding as seeing this kind of dog in action. On the other hand, there is nothing funnier than the retriever turned inside out: the comic fellow who runs away from you or brings things back just out of reach.

In reality, there is not too much distance between the cooperative retriever and the ham. Both are thinking of their owner when they have something in their mouth. The Good Retriever has been taught to share. Mister Comedian has been taught that treasures are best kept to oneself. Of course, not everybody loves a comedian.

It's a Gene Thing

The instinct to retrieve is all in the genes. For example, my Labrador Retriever Calvin would retrieve until I was begging him for a break. My Husky Kyia, on the other hand, would show me the funniest expression when I tossed a ball for her. If she could talk, I'm sure she'd say to me, "And you expect me to bring that back to you? Not!"

If you're sitting across from a dog who won't fetch your ball, don't feel bad. Some dogs were called for other wonders. In truth, I could have trained Kyia to retrieve, but I would have had to use unnatural or harsh methods. In her lifetime I never forced Kyia to do anything that didn't agree with her natural instincts.

Labrador Retrievers will fetch through rain, snow, sleet, hail, and water.

There also are exceptions to the gene rule. In fact, I know a purebred Husky who would put most retrievers to shame.

Of course, there are other dogs with the genes and the potential to make good retrievers who won't give the ball back to you. Many have elevated the game of Keep Away to an art. If this is your pal, there's hope. To teach a full retrieve—go out, bring it back and give it up—each of the steps must be taught individually before they're brought together.

Bring It Back

Anything a dog puts in his mouth is special, at least to him. So the first step in teaching the retrieve is to get your dog psyched to show you his "treasure." All your dog must do to learn this step is come back with his prize. The focus here is on the Bring, not the Give.

➤ Line up several toys, a clicker if you're using one, and treats.

➤ Gently toss a toy a few feet away from you. Each time your dog brings you a toy, shower him with praise but don't take the toy away.

➤ As your dog catches on and trots back to you happily, say "Bring."

➤ When your dog arrives, toy in mouth, praise and pet him heartily (click and treat if you like), leaving the object in his mouth. Return to your stack and toss a different toy.

➤ If your dog ignores you when he gets the toy, try running away from him after he's picked it up. If he still won't bring it back, pretend to eat some of his treat. When he brings it over, shower him with love but don't reach for the toy just yet.

➤ After your dog is bringing his toy in on the Bring command, you're ready for step two: Give.

Hand Signals
Eventually your dog must be able to do this on voice command alone. When starting out, you can use a waving motion with your right arm—an invitation to come on over.

Give It Up

Parting is such sweet sorrow. Relinquishing an object is the trickiest part of the retrieve, especially if you've chased your dog for things in the past. Be patient. Follow the steps and be smart enough not to lose your temper if your dog is trying to outsmart you. A graceful retreat is not a failure.

Give With Treats

No more chasing. That's final. Instead, offer something better.

➤ Pull up a chair and line up your clicker, some treats, and your dog's favorite toy.

➤ Call your dog over, show him the toy and praise him when he takes it.

➤ Next, with a treat and clicker in hand, say "Give." The treat should induce him to drop the toy. Click and reward the second he releases it.

Hand Signals
Hold your open palm in front of your dog's mouth.

➤ Now go to a hallway or an enclosed space. Toss the toy.

➤ Praise your dog the moment he picks it up, go to him and say "Give" as you click and reward the release.

You may notice that your dog releases the ball as you approach or tosses it on the ground near you. Although this is acceptable when starting out, you'll eventually need to be more selective with your rewards. Deliveries are to be made mouth to hand. Here's how to shape this behavior:

➤ Go back to your chair.

➤ Give your dog the toy and say "Give" as you extend your hand under your dog's mouth.

➤ If your dog tosses it on the ground, ignore the result and begin again.

➤ Click and reward the moment the toy drops into your hand.

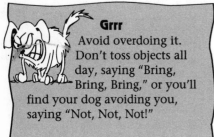

Grrr
Avoid overdoing it. Don't toss objects all day, saying "Bring, Bring, Bring," or you'll find your dog avoiding you, saying "Not, Not, Not!"

Give Without Treats

Some dogs are so food obsessed that they can't think of anything else. If this sounds like your fellow and you're having a rough time getting his attention with treats around, you'll need to teach him without treats.

It's not so hard. Follow the steps outlined previously, simply inserting an extra helping of praise where it says to click and reward with a treat.

Bring and Give

Once your dog learns that when you say "Bring," you want the object you pointed to and when you say "Give," it's a hand delivery you're looking for, you're ready to connect the two talents.

Sarah Says
Is your dog so mouthy that he's into carrying anything that moves, including your undergarments, remote control, or soap? Place treat cups throughout the house and each time he steals, shake the cup and encourage Bring. Now you'll have a resident delivery service instead of a one-dog wrecking crew.

➤ Go to a hallway or enclosed space.

➤ Give the toy a short toss and instruct "Bring". When your dog grabs it, cheer him back to you.

➤ Extend your hand to retrieve the object, Give, and reward your dog for a job well done! Repeat this twice, and then quit while you're ahead.

➤ If your dog gets so excited that he can't hold onto the toy, you might be rushing it. Go back to the earlier steps and progress slowly.

Retrieving Dowels and Dumbbells

If you plan to enter your dog in an Obedience competition, you'll need to be a bit more formal with your choice of toys to play with; actually, serious competitors would be hesitant to call the equipment they use toys. To be specific, you'll need to practice with dowels and dumbbells.

A dowel is a piece of wood shaped like a stick, but is more regular in shape and uniform in length. The dumbbell used in formal Obedience work looks like a small dumbbell you'd find at your gym, but it's made of wood.

Start your formal retrieving work with a dowel. Take your dog into a quiet room and line up your clicker, some treats, and your dowel. Again we'll break down the exercise into parts, but this time we'll go in reverse.

Take It

Present your dog with the dowel and say "Take It." If he takes it, praise him, click, and reward. (This step may take some time and some enticing. Make that dowel look interesting!) Soon your dog will take it readily. Now you're ready for the second step.

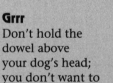

Grrr
Don't hold the dowel above your dog's head; you don't want to encourage jumping.

Hold

Now ask your dog to Hold the dowel as you put it in front of his muzzley mug. At first he'll probably spit it out; ignore that. Present the dowel again and hold it gently in his mouth as you repeat "Hold." Click and reward.

Slowly progress until your dog holds the dowel for thirty seconds. Don't worry if the seasons change while you're perfecting this exercise. I had a Collie who took almost six months to fully grasp it.

Most dogs think the dowel is just another chew toy. That's why I like to start with the dowel (so you can break the habit) before you start working with the dumbbell.

Hand Signals
When you ask your dog to Hold, point your finger close to his nose.

When your dog starts to roll the dowel in his mouth and chew, use your gentle discouraging words, "Ep, ep." If that doesn't impress him, snap his leash gently, "Ep, ep," and don't click and reward. Don't get mad, however, or you'll discourage your dog from ever retrieving for you again.

Before progressing to the next step, introduce your dog to the dumbbell. It will feel funny at first (the ends are weighted), and your dog may roll it around in his mouth, but discourage this with a light "Ep, ep."

> ### Bet You Didn't Know
>
> Dumbbells come in different sizes. Make sure the one you buy fits your dog properly. Tell the sales clerk how big your dog is and he or she should be able to help you.

Send

Now you'll need to teach your dog to go out and retrieve the dumbbell for you. In previous games you conditioned him to think retrieving was cool, so this step shouldn't a big deal.

➤ Begin by holding the dumbbell level with the dog's face and about a foot away from him. Tell your dog "Take It," encouraging him to reach for the dumbbell.

➤ Work the two-inch rule, lowering the dumbbell toward the floor two inches at a time. Encourage your dog to Take It on command each time.

➤ When you get to the floor, keep your hand under the dumbbell and shake it lightly. Release it after your dog takes it quickly, and slowly return to a standing position.

➤ Next, put your dog in a Stay, place the dumbbell in front of you on the floor, then send him to Take It. The one-foot rule is the name of this game. Have the dog Stay, put the dumbbell down one foot away, then return to him and command "Take It."

➤ Move the dumbbell out one foot at a time. Once you're three feet away, you'll find that you can progress more quickly.

Carry This, Carry That

Back when I had an office in town, it was a common spectacle to see my Labrador Calvin walking at my side carrying my lunch bag. Everybody joked that the bag was empty, but I'd bet my business and prove it was chock full of the usual lunch delicacies: turkey, chips, cookies. What they didn't know was that I made a deal with Calvin: "You carry my lunch for me and I'll give you a piece of the sandwich."

Now that your dog has learned his retrieving exercises, let's teach him the fine art of Carry.

➤ Put a raw potato in a lunch sack.

➤ Put your dog in a Sit.

➤ Fold the top of the bag crisply, turn to your dog and tell him "Carry," as you offer the bag.

➤ When he grasps the bag (which may take him a while in the beginning), praise him, click, and treat. Quit while you're ahead.

➤ An hour or two later go back and ask him to Carry again, this time stepping back and encouraging him to follow you. When he's taken a step, say "Give," reward, and praise. Repeat this lesson three times.

➤ Next put your dog on a leash and go to a hallway or open area in your house or garage. Present the bag, command Carry, and walk along five steps. If your dog drops the bag, ignore it and quit. No attention for 15 minutes. (Next time lower your goal— reward two steps.)

Hand Signals
The Carry signal is the same as the Hold signal; point in front of your dog's nose.

➤ Continue to increase the number of steps until your dog follows you around the house.

➤ Now you're ready to go outside. Start at the potato in the bag step, praising your dog a few steps at a time.

Once your dog reliably carries the bag, you can discourage a distracted drop by saying "Ep, ep," then pointing to the bag. Stay upbeat and positive. No dog wants to carry things for a grump.

When your dog has learned this trick with a bag, he'll want to carry other things, too. He'll insist on helping with the groceries; just give him a cereal box or the buns, tell him "Carry" and off to the kitchen for both of you. When it's time to clean, ask your dog to carry the rag or the paper towels. You'll both be happy.

Fetch the Paper

Wouldn't it be nice to stay inside, cozy in your pajamas, while your best furry friend happily braves the morning cold to fetch your paper? Just be careful what you wish for; a dog who's trained to fetch the paper won't discriminate. You may end up with twenty newspapers on your stoop and twenty angry neighbors!

➤ Fold a section of your newspaper over and tape it securely.

➤ Tempt your dog with it, praising any interest whatsoever.

➤ When your dog lights up to the sight of the paper, begin to command "Fetch the Paper," and let the dog take it in her mouth.

➤ If your newspaper comes in a plastic bag, introduce it to your dog next. Place the folded (and worn) paper in its plastic bag and repeat the above steps.

Grrr
Avoid sending your dog out into an unconfined area. Even the most well-trained dog has one temptation that will override all his training.

Hand Signals
Whether sending your dog out to get the paper or signaling her to deliver a message, send her off with a happy swoosh!

Sarah Says
When first playing Hide and Seek, have everyone in visual range. Slowly start to spread out until everyone is standing in different areas of the house.

Now you can take your show outside. The next morning take your dog with you on leash. When you come across the paper (which should be similar to the one you've been practicing with indoors) act surprised and point to it, saying "Fetch the Paper." If your dog picks it up, trot back to the house and don't look at her until you're ready to take it. Have a big treat waiting and praise your dog enthusiastically.

When your dog carries the paper back for you, you're ready to start sending her from the door.

➤ Initially, walk within three feet of the paper and say "Fetch the Paper."

➤ If your dog looks confused, run forward, shake the paper playfully, run back, and repeat the command.

➤ Progressively increase your distance from the paper.

➤ Each time your dog returns the paper to you, make a big fuss!

Four-Footed Fax

I was first taught this trick back in college by my big brother, John. He and his wife have an English Springer Spaniel named Chelsea who delivers notes to anyone in the house. Just write out the note, fold it up, tell Chelsea who it was meant for and off she'll go, note in mouth.

Play Hide and Seek (see Chapter 7 for that one) with two or more people in your house. Equip everyone with a treat cup. Tell your dog "Go Find Mom" and have mom call out. When the dog gets to mom, tell him "Go Find Sally" and have Sally give a yell. And so on. Once your dog learns who everyone is, you can phase out the yell from the person being found. Soon your dog will know everyone by name!

The Least You Need to Know

➤ Not every dog is a natural retriever, but most dogs can be taught to retrieve if you approach the lessons with patience and understanding.

➤ To teach a full retrieve—go out, bring it back and give it up—each of the steps must be taught individually before they're brought together.

➤ Never chase your dog to get him to give up an object. Instead, teach the Give command and be patient!

Chapter 13

At Your Service

In This Chapter

➤ Take your dog on laundry patrol

➤ Pick up the trash

➤ Turn out the lights

➤ A helping paw when you sneeze

➤ Send your dog for a soda

Now that you've perfected your dog's retrieving skills, you can put them to work. And, unlike the spouse or the kids, your dog won't think you're a nag; he'll view all the chores as one big game and rush to get started.

Collect the Laundry

The idea of this trick is that when you say "Laundry Round Up," your dog will go to each room, collect the dirty clothes and put them in the basket. Miraculous! For props, you'll need a plastic laundry basket and some laundry.

Sarah Says
This chapter gets pretty complicated. Clickers really help your dog put it all together. Check Chapter 3 for an explanation of how to use a clicker, and the form at the back of the book for how to order one.

If your dog is a laundry thief you might be somewhat pessimistic, but hear me out. Laundry bandits are often the top candidates for this task. After all, they're already interested. All you need to do is redirect their efforts. Whatever fetishes are on your retriever's list, you can trust him now because he has learned the exhilaration of sharing his prizes.

You need to start this trick by teaching your dog a few vocabulary words. Get together with a few pieces of clean laundry and the basket. Bring your dog to the basket and say "Round Up." Next, show him a sock and say "Laundry." Try it a few times a be patient; remember, you're teaching your dog a foreign language.

Here's your little helper hard at work with the laundry.

Now we'll separate the steps. First the laundry. You teach this part standing next to the basket.

➤ Place a sock on the floor three feet away from you and tell your dog "Laundry" as you point to the sock.

➤ If he's clueless, lift it up, put it in his mouth, and run backward repeating "Laundry."

➤ When you get him to bring it back to you, click and praise, letting him drop the sock at your feet.

➤ Continue to practice with laundry items, spread around the room. At first, place one item, then two, then three, sending your dog with the command Laundry each time and clicking and praising each retrieval.

Now you're ready to move on to the Round Up part of this trick.

➤ With your dog at your side and your laundry basket at your feet, give the sock to your dog as you say "Laundry."

➤ Guide his head over the basket as you say "Round Up" and click simultaneously.

➤ Though you may need a few tries to get it right, click the instant your dog drops the sock into the laundry basket.

Grrr
Do not handle the sock. Your dog will think Laundry means a mouth-to-paw delivery.

➤ Repeat this step until your dog begins to put two and two together.

➤ Now position the laundry three feet away from you. Send your dog by saying "Laundry" and when he gets it say "Round Up" (you might help a little by pointing to the basket).

➤ Initially, if your dog gets the laundry, brings it over but misses the basket, click to reward his effort. Once he's consistent, only click proper deliveries.

➤ Now try standing across the room from the basket and sending your dog, pointing at the basket and saying "Laundry" and "Round Up."

➤ Gradually progress to more pieces of laundry in the same room, then aim for a housewide round up.

Sarah Says
Got a small fry? Too small, in fact, to place her head over the Round Up basket? Cut a hole large enough for your dog to fit through into the side of a plastic basket.

Got a big house and rooms and rooms of dirty clothes? You can send your dog out on clothes patrol; just start introducing him to the concept one room at a time. Start your progression in the rooms closest to the Round Up basket and work your way up.

Pick Up the Trash

After your dog has learned how to pick something up and put it in a basket, the possibilities for turning her into a top-notch housekeeper really expand. Picking up the trash is a natural. The goal here is that when you say "Trash It," your dog will go out and pick up whatever trash she sees and put it in a trash can or bag.

Is this another request that leaves you speechless? Has your dog spent most of his life pulling trash *out* of the bin, rather than putting things *in* it? Once your pal has learned to retrieve properly you can trust him around anything, including the garbage.

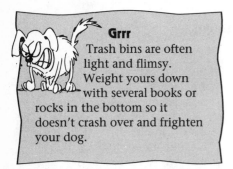

Grrr
Trash bins are often light and flimsy. Weight yours down with several books or rocks in the bottom so it doesn't crash over and frighten your dog.

For props, you'll need a trash bin with a flip top that's sized for your dog. It should be four inches lower than his chin. You'll also need some trash that's safe for him to handle—no sharp edges or food items, please.

As with all these complex tricks, we'll break this one down and teach it in parts. You start by introducing your dog to the trash can and saying "Trash."

➤ You can encourage your dog's interest in the trash can by rubbing some butter or peanut butter along the inside edge of the lid.

➤ When your dog makes contact with the trash can, click, repeat "Trash," and reward.

➤ Progressively encourage your dog to flip the lid. Remember to click and reward the instant your dog flips the lid.

Your little garbologist! Now that your dog knows how to flip the trash can lid, add some trash. Start with an easy-to-handle trashable like an old Cracker Jack box or, for your small fry, an empty gum wrapper.

➤ Place the garbage on the floor several feet from you and tell your dog "Trash It" as you encourage him to take the item.

➤ When your dog picks the garbage up, step back toward the can, extend your hand for his prize, and click and reward his retrieval. Repeat this step until your dog will go out a distance to retrieve the garbage.

➤ Try introducing more than one piece of garbage.

Now comes the hard part: getting your dog to place the garbage into the can.

➤ Start at the can, leaving the flip lid off. Place the garbage into your dog's mouth and say "Trash It," leaning over the garbage with your clicker.

➤ Your dog will probably look confused. Gently help him place his head over the trash bin (just like you did with the laundry basket). If you find him hopeless and frustrated after a few goes, just be patient.

➤ Click every attempt initially, then fade off and reinforce only those drops that are on target.

➤ Now place trashables around the room and send your dog out for them one at a time, pointing to each object and saying "Trash It." Reinforce each delivery with a click and a treat.

Now let's finish this trick by getting your dog to push the lid open and drop the garbage in. Sprinkle some trash around the room and don't worry—your pal will take care of it!

➤ Go back to standing next to the trash bin, this time with the flip lid on.

➤ Point to each piece of garbage and instruct your dog to Trash It.

➤ Help him out initially, rewarding each entry. You know he'll catch on eventually.

Grrr
Never move on to the next step of a trick before your dog has completely mastered the previous step. If you try to rush ahead before your dog is ready, you'll both just end up frustrated and unhappy.

Turn Out the Light

Do you ever have those moments when you're just too tired to get up and turn out the light? You don't need to rush out and buy The Clapper—your very own Wonder Dog is here. All you have to do is teach him to flip a switch or pull a cord when you say "Lights Out."

This trick has a lot of parts, so be patient. Make Lights Out a project the two of you can work on over time. And remember, the two cardinal rules of trick training are always be patient and always have fun.

Sarah Says
You may want to cover the area around the light switch with cardboard so your dog doesn't accidentally scratch the wall during training.

Flip the Switch

First you need to teach your dog to put his paws on the wall. Tap the wall, say "Up," and encourage any motions in that direction with clicks and praise. Most dogs catch on to this part pretty quickly, since they love to jump up anyway. (You've already taught your little trickster that jumping is by invitation only, right?)

If your pal is too little to reach the light switch, put a chair against the wall. Pat the chair and tell the dog "Up." Once he's up there, reward him. Now pat the wall and give the Up command again. Got it?

Keep practicing Up while we move on to the next part, which is teaching your dog to use his paw to flip the switch. Remember Paw way back in Chapter 7? Your dog has this one down cold, right? Remind him by asking for Paw in odd places; when your dog is lying down or standing, for example.

A dog is way more fun than The Clapper!

Now teach him Paw It by giving the command while you point to something such as a spot on the floor or a piece of paper in your hand. If your dog seems confused when you first ask, hold out your hand in the usual Paw fashion, Paw a bit, then remove it at the last minute. Puppy see, puppy do.

Now you're ready for the wall.

➤ Stand right next to the light switch and tell your dog Up as you pat the wall, positioning him so his paw is right under the light switch.

➤ Point to the switch and say "Paw It."

➤ Help him turn the switch off by gently guiding his paw. Click and warmly praise whenever he hits the wall in the right area.

➤ Keep practicing, eventually dropping your helping hand but still praising when his paw hits the wall.

➤ Eventually, reward only for correctly pawing the light switch.

Now it's time to add the Lights Out command. Start by linking it to the two commands your dog already knows. Pat the wall and say "Up, Lights Out." Then command "Paw It, Lights Out." When your dog is performing consistently, you can gradually drop the Up and Paw It commands.

Now you're ready to test your dog when you're not standing at his side. Send him from three feet, then six feet, then across the room—Lights Out! The final test? Send him from the comfort of your bed. Good night.

Sarah Says
Initially, when your dog is randomly slapping the wall with his paw, flick the light out yourself before you praise him. If you're using a clicker, click the instant the light goes out, whether by paw or hand.

Pull the Cord

Still have the old pull cords on your lights? Don't worry, your dog can learn this, too. First get a similar pull string and knot the end of it. Dangle it in front of your dog and say "Lights Out." If he reaches for it, give it a quick tug, then click and reward. Continue this until your dog grabs it quickly and releases after the tug.

This trick also works for a lamp with a pull cord. But to ensure your dog doesn't pull the string out or send your lamp flying, reward only short tugs. If your dog yanks the cord or tries to "kill" it, say "Ep, ep" and try again. If you're working with a lightweight lamp, secure it before you start practicing.

Now it's time to introduce your dog to the real thing.

Sarah Says
Is your dog uninterested in your string? Is he thinking you've confused him with your cat? Soak the string in some chicken broth.

➤ Show your dog the light and wave the string.

➤ Say "Lights Out."

➤ When your dog reaches for it, reinforce the behavior by pulling the string yourself, clicking and rewarding.

➤ Progressively reward more and more interaction with the string, always remembering to reward *after* the light is out, until your dog is pulling the cord himself.

➤ Remember to reward only gentle pulls.

Achoo!

You've got two options with this trick, which basically involves fetching a tissue from the tissue box.

1. When you say "Tissue," your dog will run and get you one.

2. When you sneeze your dog will get you a tissue.

Let me warn you that although the second option is way more impressive, it might leave your dog in a state of career stress. After all, other people sneeze, too.

Sarah Says
Three key points before you get started:

Secure the box to a low table, using tape or string.

Keep the box in one location; avoid moving it around.

Loosen the tissue for training by pulling it out and lightly restuffing it.

For props, you'll need a box of tissues, of course. Also, go to your local discount store and get one of those fancy plastic tissue box containers, so the box will have some resistance when your dog fetches the tissue. (You can also weigh down a regular box, although I had a hard time finding weights small enough.)

Step one is teaching your dog to put her front paws on the table. Pat the table and give the Up command. Click and reward the instant your dog's front paws hit the table. Be patient; just getting your dog to believe you're inviting her to come up on the table may take a while.

Make sure your dog understands it's front paws only on the table. You can discourage her from bringing the rest of her doggy self along with a gentle "Ep, ep" or even a mild restraint at first.

While I recommend using a low table, even that may not be low enough for your very small trickster. Use a low stool or chair, or even a pillow to help your little dog reach the table. Place the stool between you and your dog, facing her. With treats in hand, command "Up" and pat the stool. If your dog jumps up, reward her immediately. Soon you can say "Up" and point without patting the chair. Then simply follow the preceding steps to teach her to put her paws on the table.

Service with a smile when you sneeze.

The next part is a classic retrieve; if you're both a little weak on this, just review Chapter 12. Got it? Okay, let's teach your dog how to retrieve a tissue.

Kneel on the floor next to your tissue box and say "Tissue," followed by a very theatrical sneeze. As you do this, ruffle the top tissue to pique your dog's interest. Reward her for taking the tissue.

Good point! Now your dog has the tissue. Not much help if you need to wipe your nose! But you both know about retrieving, so once your dog takes tissues from you or off the floor, encourage Bring and Give. Reward the instant your dog drops the tissue in your hand.

Once your dog knows the command Tissue and reliably gives it back to you, you're ready to put the whole act together. Sit down and place the tissue box between your knees.

➤ Tell your dog "Get Me a Tissue," or sneeze your most wonderful sneeze, and hold out the box.

➤ Reward her the instant she grasps the tissue, the little genius!

➤ Progressively reward only proper tissue pulls, where she pulls the tissue all the way out of the box and drops it in your hand.

➤ Now set the box on the corner of the table (the place it will always be when you do this trick) and repeat the above steps. Your dog may need a gentle reminder of "Up," but you can soon phase out that command.

➤ Slowly move yourself farther and farther away from the table. Then request "Get Me a Tissue" standing and sitting in various places in the room. Be sure to reward—and say "Thank you."

Get Me a Soda

I saved the hardest for last. In this one, your long-range goal is that, from anywhere in the house, you can say "Get Me a Soda" and your dog will run to the refrigerator, open it, get a can of soda, close the refrigerator, and bring the soda to you.

It's actually not *too* tough to teach, if you break it down. Perfect one piece of this trick at a time, and your dog and you will have fun piecing it all together.

Step one is carrying a can. The best way I've found to teach this trick is to first wrap the soda can in a cotton cloth. This is a basic retrieving exercise, and you teach it the same way you taught your dog to retrieve a dumbbell in Chapter 12. First teach your dog to hold the can, then carry it, then bring it to you from a distance—in that order. Each time you present the can say "Soda." Once your dog is comfortable with the can in her mouth, begin to cut the cloth down piece by piece.

Step two is opening the refrigerator. This sounds trickier than it is, although this part, too, needs to be broken down into smaller increments.

➤ Cut a piece of rope long enough so that when it is hung in a loop from the refrigerator door handle, it will hang at the level of your dog's chin.

Grrr
Don't let your dog swing from the rope or shake it like a stubborn rat. If you do, you may ask for a soda and end up with the refrigerator door. Reward only gentle pulls. Correct hard yanks with a "No Sir."

➤ Let your dog sniff, taste, and otherwise get to know the rope, then secure it to the handle.

➤ Jiggle the rope in front of her nose and command "Get Me."

➤ Click and reward your dog the instant she grasps the rope.

➤ Next, reward a slight pull.

➤ When your dog catches on, reward only when she pulls hard enough to open the door.

Now it's time to teach your dog to remove the can from the fridge.

➤ Wrap the same can you've used for practice back up in the original cloth, and place it on a shelf that's roomy enough and high enough for your dog to comfortably grasp it in her mouth.

➤ Prop the refrigerator door open and lead your dog into the kitchen.

➤ Act truly surprised and happy to find the can in the fridge and say "Soda" in a clear, enthusiastic voice. Point it out if your dog doesn't see it right away.

➤ Reward your dog even if her attempts to retrieve the soda are less than perfect. If she drops it on the ground, encourage her to pick it up.

➤ Continue to practice until your dog is successful at each attempt to get the soda off the shelf.

Sarah Says
Always place the soda cans in the same place. Moving them onto another shelf will make it difficult or impossible for your dog to retrieve for you. Also, if you buy a six pack remove the plastic holding it together and cut it up before you throw it out (the animals of the world will thank you).

Now you and your little genius are ready to put it all together. Drum roll please.

➤ Approach the refrigerator with your dog.

➤ Jiggle the rope and *slowly* say "Get Me a...."

➤ Wait until your dog is pulling the door open to say "Soda."

➤ If she seems confused, show her the can and say "Soda."

➤ Click and reward the instant your dog hands you the soda. This is the time for jackpot treats. Mission accomplished!

Now that your dog's figured out all the steps, it's time to test her English comprehension. Stand at the fridge and command "Get Me a Soda." Is she confused? Not sure what all the words mean when they're squashed together? Don't get frustrated. Enunciate each word slowly and help your dog through the process. Continue to work through this procedure until she's got it mastered.

Progressively extend your distance from the fridge until you can ask your dog from another room. Now imagine lying on the couch, watching the game. You call out "Get Me a Soda," and here comes your dog, can in mouth. She *is* your best friend!

The cutest waiter on earth, and he's all yours!

The Least You Need to Know

> ➤ All of these tricks are based on the retrieve, so make sure you and your dog understand the tricks in Chapter 12 before you try the ones in this chapter.

> ➤ Every prop you use must be the right size for your dog. Don't ask a Chihuahua to drop something in a laundry basket that's taller than he is or a Great Dane to remove a can of soda from the smallest shelf in your fridge.

> ➤ The two cardinal rules of trick training are always be patient and always have fun.

> ➤ The most reassuring truth about all this is that helping you out is heaven to your dog. You are fulfilling every canine's wish to be truly needed.

Chapter 14

Vaudeville Vanities

In This Chapter

➤ Dancing dogs in all their glorious variations

➤ Stringing together several old tricks to make some new ones

➤ Digging a Trench, Run for Cover, Crazy Eights, and more

Now that your dog has discovered her inner talents, is she feeling full of life, full of spirit, full of herself? This chapter is for her—and you. Each of these tricks require a dog with a strong, outgoing personality and a spitfire attitude about conquering anything new. From disco dog to a theatrical death scene, the dog who masters these tricks will soon be demanding a personal agent.

Dancing Dog

Is your dog just as happy on two paws as she is on four? Is she a ham? A show-off? If your answer is "yes, yes, yes," have I got a trick for you!

If you've got a company jumper, this is also a useful trick; you can teach her that dancing is a better option. When she learns the routine, save it for homecomings or when company calls.

Grrr
Dancing is not a trick for growing pups. It can wreak havoc on their growth plates.

Grrr
There is one penalty for your Rhythmic Rover: Touching your body, or anyone else's. If your dog bumps into you while dancing say "Ep, ep" and withdraw the treat. Look up at the ceiling for five seconds, then start again.

➤ Gather some treats and a clicker, if you have one.

➤ Give your dog a hearty scratch and lots of praise to loosen her up.

➤ Hold a treat at arm's length just inches above your dog's nose.

➤ When she rises to snatch it, say "Dance" and let it go. Do this five times, then quit with a jackpot.

➤ Wait until the next day for lesson two.

➤ Take the treat and hold it just above your dog's nose, as before, but when she reaches up for it lift it an inch (or more for larger dogs) higher and say "Dance," then let it go.

➤ After three days of this routine, begin to say "Dance" as you signal your dog with the treat. Pause, increasing the amount of time before rewarding.

Disco Dog

If your dog loves to jam and you're into disco music, dust off your record collection and clear the floor. You'll never dance alone again (or be kidded about your Bee Gees infatuation).

As you're hustling around, your dog will be getting excited and wondering what part she can play in all this fun. Take one of her treats and say "Dance, Disco," then simply show her the moves you'd like her to imitate. Reward even her simplest efforts. Soon you'll notice that your dog is moving to the grooving.

The Two-Step

Are you a country music buff? There's a dance for you, too. Teach your dog the two-step. When your dog's in the proper dancing position, up on his hind legs, move the treat forward two dog-steps at a time. Be patient if he has a hard time walking at first. You did too.

May I Have This Dance?

I have a young person in my class with a dog we all call Butter, short for Butterscotch. Butter is yellow Labrador Retriever who has graduated from a wild and gregarious pup to a fine four-pawed gentleman.

One thing Butter and his owner do when they perfect a routine is dance. But it's not the dancing I've described here. No, they dance they way our parents did, paw-in-arm. It's quite a sight.

Not all dogs qualify for this routine. Your dog must be tall enough, for starters. Sure I dance around with my friend's Pug cradled in my arms, but that's different.

If your dog can reach you at least above your waist, then you have to see if he's willing to keep up with you. Pat yourself and give the Up command you both learned in Chapter 13. Then gently hold your dog's front paws (or place them on your shoulders if you have a Great Dane) and command "Dance." Step back one or two steps at a time and build up slowly. At first, please don't try to make your dog walk backward. And no Waltzes or Tangos on day one.

Grrr

If your dog's a diehard jumper who just can't seem to keep his paws off you, rethink this paw-in-arm dancing routine. Sure, it's fun, but you won't be able to get your little Casanova to stop.

Break Dance

I'll tell you how I came to this trick. A year ago I was trying to teach Beauty, my Bulldog student, the Down command. Whenever she heard Down she'd flip over, belly up, and twist around like a silly worm. Since it was too hard to get serious with her, I started saying "Break Dance" whenever she'd get started. Before long dear Beauty was break dancing on command.

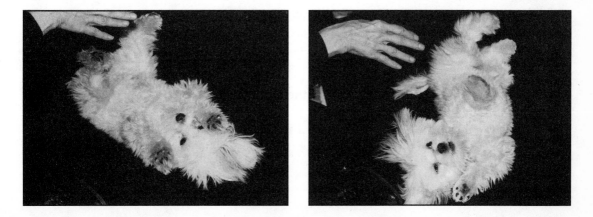

Have you ever seen anything cuter than a Maltese break dancing?

There's a prerequisite to teaching your dog this command: She must feel comfortable with her feet in the air.

➤ Encourage your dog into the proper Break Dance position by sitting on the floor and scratching her belly.

Sarah Says
Small dogs need more security when learning to Break Dance, although they're able to roll around on the floor like the big guys once they learn. Initially, extend your legs in front of you on the floor and sandwich your dog between your calves.

➤ As soon as those paws are airborne, start waving your hands above her feet and say "Break Dance."

➤ Immediately reinforce your dog with enthusiastic praise and treats. She won't know what you're doing at first, but stick with it. Soon she'll be imitating your movement.

➤ As soon as she catches on, it will be hard to get her to stop.

➤ Now try giving her the Break Dance command from a standing position.

Shoot-Out at the OK Corral

This is where we put together two tricks you learned in Chapter 8: Ask Nicely and Go to Sleep. Together they create a cool stunt that will wow audiences everywhere.

First, get your dog to sit up (Ask Nicely), adding a command such as "Put 'em Up." Make the shape of a gun with your thumb and index finger and point it at her. Practice that quite a few times.

Remember the way to teach a new command for an old trick is to first link them, then phase out the old command. So when your dog starts you'll give her the commands "Ask Nicely, Put 'em Up." Emphasize the new hand signal, and slowly eliminate the Ask Nicely command.

Once your dog is sitting up, it's time for the Go to Sleep command. Link it with Bang, as you "pull the trigger" on your hand gun. If she has trouble, gently help her over to her side. Often the dog will get so excited that she will fall down anyway. Practice the two steps together several times, rewarding for each improvement and phasing out Go to Sleep.

 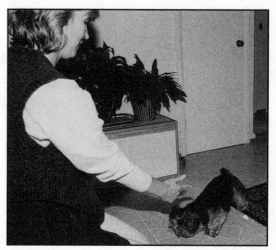

Okay partner, put 'em up!   *Bang!*

Now to put it all together.

➤ Put your dog in a Sit-Stay.

➤ Stand three feet away and command "Put 'em Up" as you take aim.

➤ Pause a few seconds and say "Bang."

➤ Mission accomplished! Now practice at progressively farther distances.

Digging a Trench

Have you considered hiring your dog out to the local excavating company? The answer, of course, is to teach her to dig. By teaching your dog to dig in specific locations, you'll be able to discourage her from digging in other places. Sound too good to be true?

➤ Equip yourself with a clicker, garden gloves, and treats.

➤ Find a private area in your yard or a local park to teach your dog to dig. Bury some treats one inch under the ground to perk her interest.

Sarah Says
I can already feel the page trembling; some of you are worried that, with your approval, your dog will unearth your shrubbery and carpets. Though I won't promise you a rose garden, most dogs who are reinforced for digging in one area usually stick to it.

➤ Start blissfully digging yourself, unearthing the treats as you go and handing them to your dog.

➤ Reward your dog for joining in, saying "Go Dig."

➤ Now try hiding a few treats or a toy before bringing your dog to her digging spot. Like an archeologist discovering treasures, she'll unearth them with obvious delight.

Run for Cover

Once your dog knows this trick she'll use it all day long, just to get your attention.

To begin, use a treat to lead your dog under the object you want her to go under (for this example we'll use a table). Each time, use the command Under. Practice this step periodically throughout the day.

Run for cover.

Now send her under the table with Under and command "Stay." Release her with Okay and a great big hug. Gradually increase the amount of time before the release.

Ready to put it all together? Get some treats and your clicker, if you have one.

➤ After sending your dog Under and instructing Stay, say "Peekaboo" as you use a treat to lure just your dog's nose out from under the table.

➤ Click and release the treat when your dog's nose is the only thing showing.

➤ If she has her whole head out, lure her head back under the table and start again.

*The delicious
Peekaboo!*

Although it may take some practice to master the perfect Peekaboo, once learned it's never forgotten.

Injured Dog

Although there are many steps to this one, broken down it's not too complicated.

➤ Gather your clicker and treats.

➤ With your dog on-leash, give the Sit command.

➤ Next, command "Paw" (your Chapter 7 favorite, right?) as you hold the index finger of your left hand under her forearm.

➤ Simultaneously, introduce the leash under her paw with your right hand.

➤ Next command "Stand" (you learned that one in Chapter 3), then "Paw." Introduce the injured dog hand signal.

➤ If your dog's confused, lift the left paw gently with your leash. Click and reward the second your dog has her paw in the air.

Hand Signals
Hold your right arm at your side, elbow bent. Then flop your hand down as if you had just broken your wrist. (Ouch!)

Practice this a lot. Got it? Okay, on to the finished production.

➤ Command "Stand," then "Paw" (give the hand signal), cradling your dog's paw with the leash.

➤ Step two feet away from her and command "Come," still supporting her paw.

➤ Remind her that her paw still needs to be off the floor by giving the hand signal several times throughout the Come. Click and reward her for a job well done.

Crazy Eights

This trick is fun for you to teach and fun for dogs of all shapes and sizes to learn. What could possibly be better than that?

➤ Start from the Heel position, take a giant step forward with your right foot only, then freeze. Point between your legs and use a treat to encourage your dog to come "Through."

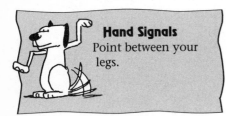

Hand Signals
Point between your legs.

➤ Once your dog has perfected Through, use the treat to lead your dog once around your legs in a figure eight pattern, ending up back in the Heel position. (Obviously, you'll have to rely solely on the lure of the treat; using a leash to lead your dog would leave you both hopelessly tangled!)

Repeat this step until you're *sure* your dog knows it well.

➤ To put it all together, do the same routine, but walk forward extremely slowly.

Sarah Says
If your dog's having trouble, do one part at a time. First through the middle, then around the right leg…reward. Then through the middle again…reward, and so on. Practice this until she does it very well.

➤ Each time your dog circles a leg, move the opposite leg forward.

➤ If that's okay with her, pick up the pace; if not, go back a step and perfect that.

➤ After some practice, she'll be tripping you and bringing the crowds to tears with laughter.

Once your dog has perfected Through, use the treat to lead him in a figure eight pattern.

The Least You Need to Know

➤ If your dog likes to jump, teach her to dance. Then save the trick for those times when jumping is a temptation.

➤ If you've got a problem digger, teach her to dig on command. It works the same way.

➤ Always practice on a surface with secure footing, such as grass or carpet.

➤ All the tricks here build on tricks and basic skills learned in previous chapters. Make sure your foundation is solid before you try to put together an act and take it on the road.

Chapter 15

The Impressionist

➤ Teach your dog to roll over, flip and catch a treat, and crawl

➤ Balancing a book on the dog's head

➤ Expanding your trick repertoire by using hand signals

Animal acts always make people smile, especially when they're all performed by *your* animal. Some of these impressions your friends will easily guess. Others will be even more funny if you announce the impression first.

The Dolphin

Who has not seen a dolphin do a perfect water roll at an aquarium or a water park? Your dog, while not as fluid in her movements, can still do a pretty fair likeness. To get started, place your clicker and treats on a nearby table.

➤ Call your dog to you and put her on a Down-Stay.

➤ Scratch your dog's belly until she lies on one side.

➤ Take a treat and hold it above your dog's ear. Now circle it slowly backward over the back of her head as you say "Roll Over."

➤ Initially your dog may need some help. Guide her over by gently pushing her top front leg to the other side as you say the command. Click and treat a full roll, whether you helped your dog or not.

➤ Repeat this four times a session, then quit on a high note with your dog's favorite game.

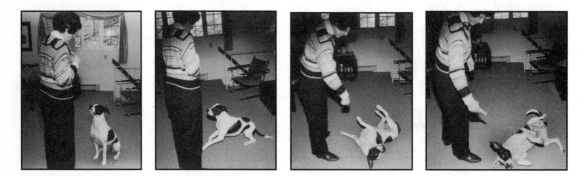

Teach your dog to do the roll, fluid as a dolphin.

Once your dog seems able to follow the command, you can teach her to jump up after each roll. For this all you need is as little bit of enthusiastic body language and up she goes. Initially you should reward the roll; then reward the roll and finish.

Now you're ready to teach your dog the hand signal for this trick. Continue to kneel next to her when commanding Roll Over, but lean backward (in the direction you want her to roll), hold your index finger parallel to the floor, and draw small circles in the air as you give your verbal command. Help your dog initially if she seems confused, praising her as you assist and jumping up with her to end the trick. Once she responds alone, stand up and give the command and the hand signal, always accentuating your hand signal.

Once your dog has learned the hand signal, you're ready for control at a distance.

Grrr

This is a very entertaining trick, but please don't force your dog if she's not into it. Some dogs love to act silly, others don't. How will you know? If your dog shifts from side to side with ease, if she rolls around on her own, she'll be game. If rolling around on the floor is beneath her standards, don't force it.

➤ Place your dog in a Down-Stay and stand back three feet. Use your hand signal, leaning your body in the direction you're sending your dog, as you command "Roll Over."

➤ If your dog looks confused, go to her calmly and help out, getting back into your starting position as she finishes the trick.

➤ When she performs on her own, give her a jackpot of treats and end with a fun game.

➤ Back up two feet at a time during your subsequent practice sessions, until your dog will Roll Over at a reasonable distance from you.

Bet You Didn't Know

Visualization helps. Create a picture in your mind of your dog performing the trick flawlessly, and keep it there while you're teaching her how.

The Seal

In this one, you teach your dog to balance a treat on her nose, then flip it up and catch it. Sound hard? We've all seen seals do this with a fish. And surely your pup is smarter than a seal!

You'll need to break this one into parts: the balance, and the flip and catch.

Balancing Act

➤ Line up treats and your clicker on a nearby table.

➤ Put your dog on a Sit-Stay.

➤ Gently hold your dog's nose steady for five seconds, reminding Stay if she gets squeamish. Click and reward just that. Repeat five times. The first lesson is over.

➤ Later that day or the next day, repeat the above lesson, but place a treat on your dog's nose while you steady it, reminding Stay.

➤ After five seconds, say "Okay," removing the treat that's on her nose and rewarding her with a different treat. *Do not reward your dog with the treat on her nose.*

➤ Repeat this exercise four times, then stop for the day.

➤ Continue to practice this step until your dog is proficient at balancing the treat on her nose for at least fifteen seconds, no nose-holding required.

Flip and Catch

Teach this part only after perfecting the balance.

➤ Balance a treat on your dog's nose, then introduce the next concept by saying "Okay" as you slide the treat from your dog's nose to her mouth.

Sarah Says
To help your dog learn to wait for your Okay before flipping the treat, vary the balance time before sliding the treat into her mouth.

➤ After a day or two you should notice that your dog tries to flip the treat herself. Praise her only if her flip follows your Okay.

➤ If she flips prematurely, say "Ep, ep" and practice the balance alone a few times before continuing.

Now you're ready to put the whole trick together.

➤ Balance the treat and command Stay.

➤ Walk back three feet and pause. Vary the length of your pauses as you practice.

➤ Say "Okay" for the catch and make a big fuss when she does, praising your dog with lots of love.

Once your dog knows how to balance a treat, he's ready to learn the flip and catch.

The Snake

This trick always amazes me, and it's fairly easy to teach. Your dog must be proficient in Down, but if you've gotten this far I'll take that for granted.

➤ Gather up your treats and a clicker.

➤ Give your dog the Down command.

➤ Hold a treat in front of his nose and bring it forward slowly so he has to stretch. As he does, say "Crawl."

➤ Progressively encourage your dog to move forward.

➤ The first few days you should reinforce one crawl step at a time.

➤ If you're having trouble teaching this one, lie in front of your dog and extend your hand so that it just reaches his nose.

➤ Wiggle your hand forward as if it were a mouse in the grass, again reinforcing the smallest attempt to reach for the treat.

➤ Once your dog will crawl forward ten feet (this might take a few weeks), begin giving your dog the Crawl command from a kneeling position.

➤ Finally, stand up and say "Crawl" as you signal him forward, wiggling your hand in front of him.

Sarah Says

If your dog's having trouble keeping her belly planted on the floor, lay your right hand across her shoulder blades and apply the least amount of pressure possible.

Think you're hot stuff? Then try this crawl routine.

➤ Place your dog in a Down-Stay and stand three feet in front. Instead of calling her, kneel down and say "Crawl."

➤ Release her with "Okay" the moment she gets to you, and celebrate. Job well done! Now you can work at getting her to crawl to you across the room. Good luck.

Bet You Didn't Know

Dogs have crawled throughout evolution. As wolves they crawled into their own dens and into the caves of other animals. As dogs they've crawled through brambles, under fences, and under the living room table with your favorite shoe.

Eliza Doolittle

Okay, this is not an animal trick. But it *is* still an impression. Do you remember the scene in *My Fair Lady* when Eliza Doolittle walks around the living room with a book balanced on her head? This is the same trick, only your dog is going to do it. As usual, let's break this trick down into its significant parts.

Stand Still

Here's a quick refresher course, in case your dog has forgotten the art of standing still.

➤ Kneel down on the floor next to your dog.

➤ Place your right hand, palm out, under your dog's buckle collar.

➤ Slide your left hand under your dog's belly.

➤ Command Stand-Stay as you gently prop your dog into a standing position.

➤ Relax your right hand and slide your left to rest on your dog's thigh.

Hand Signals
The hand signal for Stand Still is a level hand, arm extended, palm up.

➤ Pause, count to five, and release with an Okay.

➤ Slowly increase the time to one minute.

➤ Now repeat the same sequence from a standing position.

➤ Begin to let go with your left hand, then your right, as you steady your dog with calm Stay commands and a relaxed posture.

Once your dog catches on, you'll find a million uses for this command: wiping muddy paws, brushing, a towel dry, an Eliza Doolittle imitation....

Slow Down

This is another little trick that I'm sure you can think of a million uses for. Plus, your dog can't possibly balance a book on his head and fly across the room at the same time. Let's slow it down!

To get started you'll need two people: one to lead the dog forward and one to hold him back.

➤ Position yourself in front of your dog with treats and your partner behind, holding a leash attached to your dog's buckle collar.

➤ Using your Stay signal, command Stand-Stay. If your dog moves, reposition her calmly and quietly.

➤ To signal your dog to move forward close your fingers, move your hand forward and say "Slowly."

➤ After each step, reward your dog with a treat as your assistant pulls gently back to stop the dog from taking more than one step at a time.

➤ Repeat this until your dog begins to slow after each step on her own; no tug necessary.

➤ Now see if you can do it without a partner, using Shhh if your dog is too excited. One step at a time.

➤ Now try it at a distance. Leave your dog in a Stand-Stay and stand three feet in front of her. Command and signal "Slowly" and praise your dog for moving with caution.

Balancing the Book

This next step is a big one. If your dog's not ready for it, slow up yourself.

Consider the type of book you use. Paperbacks sag and don't balance well. Avoid books with jackets or glossy covers—too slippery. A bare, hardcover book works best. Also, use a book that doesn't weigh too much and that suits the size of your dog; your Chihuahua may only be able to handle a book of postage stamps.

➤ To help your dog learn to balance a book, you will have to steady her head so the book rests evenly. Do this by gently holding her muzzle with your right hand, giving the Stay signal with your left hand in front of her nose and repeating "Stay."

➤ At first, click and reward after just a few seconds, building the duration slowly over many days.

➤ When your dog begins to learn the routine, lift your right hand off her muzzle ever so slightly as you leave the Stay signal in place and remind "Stay."

➤ Slowly increase the time your dog can balance the book without your help and the distance you can move from her.

> **Sarah Says**
> Is your dog letting the book slide? Either you're going too fast or your dog is following you with her eyes as you step away. Help her keep her focus steady by holding the hand signal for Stay steady at nose level, then moving it slightly up or down if she needs recentering.

Putting It All Together

If I had to pick the toughest trick in the book, this would be it. So drum roll, please. Here goes.

➤ Standing close to your dog, place her in a Stand position and tell her to Stay.

➤ Place the book on her head, remind Stay and step away two feet.

➤ Keeping your Stay signal level with your dog's nose, command "Slowly" and give the hand signal.

➤ Immediately remove the book after one step, click and reward. Quit on a high note and go for a walk.

➤ Work on this step for a few days to build your dog's confidence. Progress to two steps, then three, four, five....

➤ Now send me a picture of your dog imitating Eliza Doolittle for the next printing of this book.

The Neighbor's Dog

This one's my favorite. Once your dog knows the hand signal for Speak, you can say "What does the neighbor's dog do?" give the signal, and your dog will bark, bark, bark.

This is a pretty funny trick, and it illustrates an important concept about hand signals: Once your dog can respond to your signals, it won't matter what you're saying. Your dog will react to the signal alone.

When you feel confident about your hand signals, you can borrow other tricks from this book to do more impressions. For example, Wolf is just the Howl command and Dancing Bear is easily done using one of the many dance routines you learned in Chapter 14.

If you want to tack on a verbal command, hook the new command onto the old (for example, Howl-Wolf) while emphasizing your hand signal.

The Least You Need to Know

➤ Difficult tricks should be broken down into parts and taught gently and with lots of patience.

➤ Balancing acts require strict concentration and a steady Stay; it's your job to help your dog get it right.

➤ Keep your training sessions short and upbeat.

➤ Hand signals are essential in helping your dog convert from one verbal command to another. Once your dog will respond to your signals, however, it won't matter what you're saying.

Pet Detective

Initially I had a hard time deciding which chapter to end the trick section with. But I decided to save the best for last. Your dog doesn't need to be a miraculous retriever or double jointed to succeed in Doggy Detective School. The only prerequisites are a curious nose and an enthusiastic heart.

Sniff and Find

To train a good detective you must start with the basics. What better to get that sniffer going than with some tasty treats?

Stage One

Good detective work begins with the basic sniff and find.

Sarah Says
Always vary the time you pause before releasing your dog, so he won't jump the gun. Pause three seconds, ten seconds, fourteen, or twenty—mix it up. This will encourage your dog to concentrate on your commands.

➤ Gather some smell-good treats, go to a large room or hallway, and place your dog in a Sit-Stay.

➤ Say "Sniff" as you hold a treat in front of your dog's nose.

➤ Discourage any test-tasting with "Ep, ep."

➤ Remind Stay, toss the treat no more than three feet in front of you, and make your dog wait.

➤ Release with "Okay, Find."

➤ Praise your dog for locating and gobbling the treat.

➤ Gradually extend your toss to not more than ten feet. Once your dog perfects this part of the trick, move on to the next stage.

Stage Two

➤ Command Sniff and Stay as before, but leave your dog's side and place the treat inches in front of him.

➤ Return to your dog's side, pause and release with "Okay, Find."

➤ Gradually extend your distance to not more than fifteen feet. At this point, your dog may lose sight of the treat and have to rely on his sniffer to find it.

Bet You Didn't Know

Unlike us, dogs have better peripheral vision than they do distance vision. That's why when you see something in front of you, your dog may not.

Stage Three

Now you're ready to put your four-footed detective to the test.

➤ Place your dog on a Stay four feet from the entrance to the room.

➤ Instruct "Sniff," remind "Stay," and place your treat *out of sight* around the corner.

➤ Return to your dog, pause and then send him off with "Okay, Find."

➤ Cheer him on if he seems confused. You may have to get on all fours yourself and sniff around, though you should praise him enthusiastically regardless of how he locates the treat.

Sarah Says
This was my dog Kyia's favorite game. I used vegetables, hiding four or five while I was making a salad, just to keep her busy.

Once your dog has the idea and is racing to put his nose to work, you can progressively hide the treat in more challenging places. And who's to say that you have to hide just one?

Find Your Toy

Now let's progress to finding something just as fun but a little less tasty: toys. For this you'll need a clicker if you use one, some good treats, and two distinctly different toys. I'll use a ball and a little stuffed cow toy, but you can use whatever toys your dog loves.

➤ Start with the ball. Hold it in front of your dog, clicker in the other hand and treats lined up on a nearby table.

➤ Say "Find Your Ball" as you hold the ball in front of your dog. When he reaches for it, click, treat, and praise.

Sarah Says
Though I encourage you to use treats initially to motivate your dog, you'll be able to phase them out as soon as your dog gets a mental image of what you're expecting.

➤ Repeat a few times, then tell your dog to Stay as you place the ball a few feet in front of him. Repeat "Find Your Ball" as you point to it. Click and reward any contact.

➤ Continue to move the ball farther from you and progress to hiding it out of sight.

➤ Practice that trick for a week, then start the whole routine from scratch with the cow. The command should be Find Your Cow.

That was the easy part. Now we're going to make it a little harder.

➤ With your dog in a Sit-Stay, place both toys in front of him, about three feet apart.

➤ Command "Find Your Cow."

➤ If your dog picks the ball, don't correct him or sound disappointed. Calmly take the toy, replace it, show your dog the cow and say "Cow." When he makes contact, click and reward.

➤ If your dog picks the cow make a big fuss; what a genius!

➤ Practice this a few times at each session, sometimes sending the dog for the ball and sometimes for the cow. (Don't alternate them; that's too easy and your dog will quickly catch on.)

➤ Progressively place the toys farther away.

Once your dog has mastered the art of association, you're ready to test his brain some more. Place one toy three feet from you, and the other ten feet away. Send your dog for the closer one at first, and then send him for the one farthest away. Switch the toys' locations and vary which one you send him to.

At this point you can apply the dog's discrimination abilities to other objects, as I'll discuss here.

Find the Keys

How much time do you spend around your house looking for your keys? It would be great if you could just send your little genius detective after them, wouldn't it? Here's how:

➤ Line up some treats, grab the keys, and round up the clicker if you use one.

➤ Place your dog in a Sit-Stay and let him sniff the keys as you say "Sniff."

➤ Toss the keys a few feet out and instruct "Find the Keys." If your dog makes contact, click immediately and reward. If not, help him out by guiding him or shaking the keys and click the second he catches on.

➤ Progressively extend the distance you toss the keys in front of you. When your dog really learns this part, you can start to hide the keys in another room.

➤ When you hide the keys, do it in plain sight and follow your dog while he searches. Reinforce with a click and/or a treat the second he locates them.

> **Sarah Says**
> Do you leave your keys all over the house? Perhaps you should consider spraying your key chain with your perfume from time to time. The better to sniff it out.

Where's the Remote?

This is, perhaps, the most often-asked question in America. And your doggy detective always knows the answer!

By this time your dog should know Sniff and Find. Line up the treats and your clicker, and let's get to work.

➤ Let your dog have a good sniff of the remote, enhancing its smell with something memorable such as baby powder.

➤ Leave him in a Stay and place the remote a few feet away.

➤ Release your dog with "Find the Remote" and reinforce any contact.

➤ Continue to increase the distance, then begin to hide it in the usual lost-remote locations.

> **Sarah Says**
> Is your dog an expert retriever? You can have your Private Eye retrieve the object once he's found it. Praise the Find, then encourage Bring.

Find Bobby

Have kids? Ever lose them? In the house, outside, at the neighbor, or elsewhere? Pet Detective to the rescue.

Start with one child, who I'll call Bobby.

➤ Place Bobby across the room with a treat cup.

➤ Take your dog across the room and say "Find Bobby."

➤ When Bobby hears his name, he should shake the treat cup.

➤ When your dog goes to Bobby, Bobby should reward him with a treat.

➤ Repeat as often as necessary, until the shaking of the cup is no longer necessary to encourage your dog to find Bobby. During the training process, Bobby should offer a treat whenever he's found.

➤ Now hide Bobby in the next room. Start back at the beginning where Bobby shakes the cup when he hears his name.

➤ Extend your distance to other rooms and locations until your dog is proficient at finding Bobby wherever he's hiding.

➤ Now practice outdoors, first with Bobby close by, and eventually with Bobby behind a tree or somewhere out of sight.

➤ You can start adding kids one at a time, until your dog knows everyone in the neighborhood.

Bet You Didn't Know

Actually, I should call this box Bet You Didn't *Notice*. However, I will admit under torture that Find Bobby is remarkably similar to Four-Footed Fax in Chapter 12. It's intentional, of course, because it illustrates an important point: The same trick can have many applications. Your dog will enjoy them all!

Snoop Doggy Dog

Though your dog won't be able to find you a refund on your taxes, he can learn to find just about anything you can lose. Dogs are able to associate plenty of objects and words. Just follow the basic framework for the tricks taught in this chapter, and initially rely on treats to reinforce his success.

Here are some other everyday things you may want to teach your dog to scout out: your slippers, the cat (you *know* the cat is going to love this one!), your other mitten—be creative. What gets lost in your home? Now, tell it to your dog. Pet Detective to the rescue!

The Least You Need to Know

➤ Introduce the object at short distances.

➤ Reward any association.

➤ Increase the distance slowly, up to fifteen feet.

➤ Initially hide the item around the corner in plain sight.

➤ Progressing to more difficult hiding places, leave a short trail to make it easier.

➤ Praise every success warmly.

Part 4
Dog Olympics

Are you feeling all tricked out? Trick after trick and the training's getting stale? There's more than one way to have fun.

In this section I'll take an in-depth look at different sporting events you and your dog can do together. Certain skills have been around for ages. Herding, sledding, hunting, and drafting are as much a part of dog evolution as fur and a tail. Other events, such as Agility, Flyball, and Frisbee, are the new sports on the block. Energizing and fun, they involve teamwork and strategy, and can be practiced alone or with other enthusiasts.

Chapter 17

Iron Dog Agility

In This Chapter

➤ What is Agility and what is it good for?

➤ Obstacle training

➤ The rules and regulations

➤ Finding or starting an Agility club

If you think you've seen everything but you haven't seen Agility, let me promise you one thing—you ain't seen nothing yet. The only thing more fun than watching Agility is doing it yourself. Similar to Grand Prix jumping for horses (though, in my opinion, more fast-paced and nail-biting exciting), this sport is good for any purebred or mixed breed dog, no matter the size or personality. Agility encourages confidence in a shy dog and teaches the wild ones self-control. Read on and discover the fun that awaits you.

What's It All About?

When I look at an Agility course—basically a large field covered with obstacles like fences, tunnels, see-saws, and tires—I see one gigantic playground. However, it's far more than an open area where dogs run haphazardly from one obstacle to another. Agility is a sport that tests a dog's ability to maneuver over and through equipment, and the human handler's ability to guide their dog along a specified route. It's a team sport, and at competition level it's scored and recorded for all to see.

This may sound like an impossible task for those of you having trouble directing your dog down the street on a leash, but don't give up hope. If your dog has energy and drive, this might be just the activity to get involved in. Giving your dog an outlet for all his energy, and teaching him a way to focus on you that allows him to have fun, may be just what the trainer ordered. A dog that is usually challenging tends to be more willing to obey while doing Agility. After all, training through obstacles for continual praise and food rewards is a lot more interesting than a walk around the block.

Sarah Says

If you've got a giant breed, understand that your dog may have trouble navigating some of the obstacles on the course. Start with the equipment that your dog is physically able and enthusiastic to try.

The best part of Agility is that it gives you time to hang out with your dog, meet other people and their dogs, and be a kid again. Of course, you won't be the one climbing see-saws or dashing over A-frames, but when you watch your dog do it you're going to wish you could.

So are you game? All dogs are invited to take part, though if your dog is overweight, physically disabled, lame, or a sworn couch potato, you'd be better off with another, less demanding activity.

You can tell if your dog is Agility material by looking at him. Is he physically sound? Does he know the basic commands like Sit, Stay, Down, and Heel? If not, you need to teach him those first. As soon as he catches on, he'll make a good candidate.

Grrr

There is one personality trait that is too challenging even for Agility: certifiable hyperactivity. Many people think they have a hyper dog when, in fact, their dog just needs exercise and structure. Certifiably hyperactive dogs can't concentrate on one thing for more than a second. If you think your dog may have a real problem, have him checked out by a veterinarian before you throw in the towel.

And I'll let you in on a little secret: Some of the best Agility dogs started out with severe behavior problems like chewing walls and excessive barking. Why? Because dogs with these kinds of behavior problems are very dependent on their owners and fuss canine-style when they're not busy. If you have an inherently good dog who just loves you a little too much, Agility may solve his problem.

Breed and size make no difference in Agility training or competition. Anything from a Chihuahua to a St. Bernard can surf the course.

How Do I Start?

To get started in Agility you'll need to find a class in your area. There are some addresses at the end of this chapter to help you get started finding a club that offers classes. Once you do, go a few times without your dog. Look, listen, and watch. Speak if you're spoken to, but initially just soak in the atmosphere. You may be the best trainer in the world, but you're in someone else's ballpark now and you have a lot to learn.

Bring copies of your dog's current inoculation records and a photo. Dog people love photos. It will endear your dog to people before they've even met.

The director of the program will probably notice you and introduce herself. When she does, tell her about your dog, your interest in joining her club, and show your inoculation records and photo. The director will appreciate your thoughtfulness.

Have a list of questions prepared.

➤ Are there special sessions to introduce beginners?

➤ Are the classes separated by age (good to find out if you plan on bringing a puppy)?

➤ What equipment should I bring? Do you suggest specific treats or toys?

➤ Does my dog have to pass an Obedience test before we come? What commands should I brush up on?

➤ How many people are allowed per dog? May family or friends come and watch?

➤ How do I handle an accident if my dog has one?

There will probably be a fee and a registration form to fill out; do this at home, before you get to class. The first day you come with your dog, stay upbeat and positive, letting him observe and keeping him at heel. Your dog's first impulse will be to sniff everything—dogs, obstacles, and people included—and although you can allow that in quiet zones, this is a good time to teach self-control.

Though you can't compete until your dog is twelve months old, you can introduce the obstacles to your

Grrr
If your dog has not been properly socialized, the first day may be a real shocker: dogs flying, people cheering, strange equipment. You may need to hang out on the sidelines for a while until your dog is more steady. Remember, your dog reacts the way you react, so stand confident and don't pet your dog until he's confident, too. Pay attention to a nervous dog and what do you get? A nervous dog.

puppy as soon as he's had all his shots. Avoid repetitions, be careful to guard your pup from falling, and use lots of treats and praise to encourage his curiosity.

Obstacles and Training

Agility equipment is broken down into six categories. Since every dog is different, yours will take to some equipment and want to skip others. The best rule is to start on the equipment your dog enjoys and work on the rest periodically, in easy-to-master steps.

When you're starting out in Agility, it's always best to start with classes. First of all, the clubs have all the equipment, and there can be a lot of it. In addition, they've had a lot of experience training dogs to do things not all dogs naturally do—and keeping it fun.

Every club will have its own ways of introducing you to its equipment. There are a few universal rules, however, that I can teach you.

1. Simplify each obstacle before approaching it with your dog. Lower the contact obstacles and the hurdles, master one or two weave poles at a time, and finish up an exhausting routine in the pause box.

2. Praise your dog warmly and lovingly every step of the way.

3. Stay positive, even when your dog isn't perfect. Initially he'll be nervous and distracted. Expect that.

Hand Signals
Use both verbal and hand signals when training your dog and teach him to respond to either. When giving signals, be consistent and direct your dog to the obstacles with a strong, clear motion using a flat palm.

4. When your dog runs around an obstacle or doesn't follow through, stay calm. Put him back on a leash, if necessary. You may need to slow down a step or two, as well. Praise your dog when he completes the exercise properly.

5. Water, water, water. Dogs dehydrate easily, especially when exercising. Some dogs have so much fun with the course that they forget to replenish themselves. Have fresh, cool, *not cold* water available for your dog (and anyone else's) every ten to fifteen minutes.

I can also give you some tips for each type of obstacle that will give you a bit of a head start.

Contact Obstacles

These are the pieces of equipment your dog will walk over or across. They include:

➤ Dog walk

➤ Cross-over

➤ See-saw

➤ A-frame

Cross-over and dog walk. I had to walk a plank once. I was playing Wendy in my second-grade production of *Peter Pan*. It was a terrifying experience.

Teaching your dog to walk narrow planks can be just as frightening initially, so have some sympathy. Make sure you have at least two spotters to ensure your dog doesn't jump or fall from the planks. If your dog is super scared, lower the plank and give your dog a treat just for being up there.

Lead your dog to the plank using the command Walk Along or Plank, and guide him slowly. This may take some time, so be patient. Once your dog braves the planks, perhaps even welcoming the challenge, begin to command your dog from a few steps back. The first few times you both brave this step, ask your spotters to hang around in case your dog loses his footing or decides to jump.

One rule on these two obstacles, and several others, is that your dog must touch a yellow contact zone at the base before jumping down. To encourage your dog to do this you can hold a reward at the bottom or teach your dog to jump through a hoop. Then, place the hoop at the base of the planks.

Cross-over

Dog walk

See-saw. The first time I saw this contraption I got a little scared. How, I thought, will my dog ever learn to navigate that thing without killing herself? Oh, how I underestimated Kyia!

Approach this exercise just like the planks, although you'll need to teach your dog to stop in the center to let the see-saw's center of gravity shift. Initially use spotters to guide your dog and hold the see-saw as it goes down.

The most important point to teach your dog is to remain on the apparatus until the see-saw is resting on the ground. Using toy and food lures, repeat this exercise at your dog's side until he's got it. Then, progressively move away as your dog perfects each stage.

See-saw

A-frame. A-frames are a formidable obstacle. Before you even let your dog sniff the thing, lower it and test its sturdiness. After exploring it with your dog, let him observe a few of his buddies going over. Next, lead him up using the command Frame It or Scramble. Initially, you should stay on the left side and hold the leash ten inches from the collar.

Have a few extra people around to guard against your dog leaping or falling off the frame. The first few times should be slow, easy, and rewarding. Pretty soon your dog will be the one wanting to speed it up.

Once your dog is comfortable, start speeding up your approach. If your dog has trouble with the descent, you can repeat the same procedure described for the cross-over and dog walk. Remember, your dog must touch the contact zone before moving on.

Once your dog has mastered the approach and exit, incrementally lift the frame to its regulation height.

A-frame

Bet You Didn't Know

There is one obstacle that dogs can't overcome in Agility. It's overgrown toenails. They can really hurt when your dog scrambles up and down the equipment. Help your dog avoid discomfort by keeping his toenails trimmed.

Tunnels

There are two tunnels you'll teach your dog to go through:

➤ Pipe tunnel

➤ Collapsed tunnel

Pipe tunnel. When working on the pipe tunnel, start with a short piece that will allow your dog to see clear through to the other side. If your dog is uneasy, let him watch other dogs going through and have a friend on the other side of the tunnel coaxing him through with a favorite toy. Reward your dog with food and praise for every successful entry.

After your dog gets the hang of it, run toward the tunnel piece and command "Tunnel" as you signal toward the obstacle and run to the other side. If your dog stops short or runs by, do not praise or look at him. Reward only complete performances.

Grr
Placing food or toys in the tunnel will encourage your dog to stop inside. Not good! Reward only enthusiastic runs all the way through.

Slowly add pieces to the tunnel. When you get to the point of the curve, go back to the beginning. Once again, let him watch other dogs practice and have a friend coach him through.

Pipe tunnel

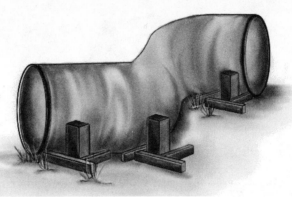

Sarah Says
In her book *Agility Training*, Jane Simmons-Moake recommends practicing with a damp chute, especially if you plan to compete. Agility competitions take place rain or shine.

Collapsed tunnel. The collapsed tunnel is a tube made of fabric that your dog must "squirt" through. Work on this one after you've perfected the pipe tunnel, using the same command and signal. At first roll up the chute and have someone hold it open.

Coach your dog through, slowly unrolling the collapsible fabric bit by bit.

Collapsed tunnel

Hurdles

There are many types of hurdles on an Agility course:

➤ Single bar jump

➤ Double bar jump

➤ Spread bar or triple bar jump

➤ Long jump

➤ Barrel jump

➤ Bone jump

➤ Optional jumps: fan, lattice wall, and water jump

Single bar jump

Double bar jump

Spread bar jump

Long jump

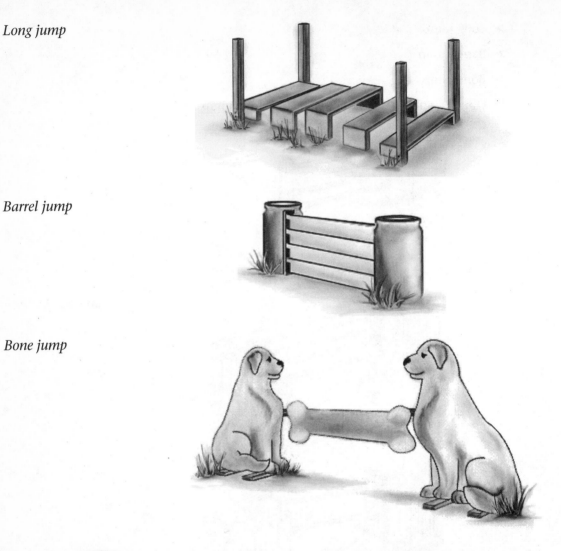

Barrel jump

Bone jump

Sarah Says

If your dog darts to the side of an obstacle, physically block that pathway when approaching it again. Don't let your dog get in the habit of repeating mistakes.

Most dogs love to jump. As a matter of fact, I'm pressed to think of any that don't. Teaching your dog to jump in an organized fashion can be both fun and challenging.

While the hurdles are all different sizes and shapes, you teach your dog to negotiate them in basically the same way. Pick one command for all the jumps. Different commands get confusing, and the action is the same for all the jumps. Simple is best.

Start on the solid jumps that your dog won't be able to sneak under. Initially, lower the jump to a height you can handle, and investigate it with your dog. With your dog on a leash, command Over or Hup and take the jump together. It's fun for you too, right?

Once your dog is comfortable, repeat the procedure off leash. Then stand beside the jump and send your dog over. Progressively back up, until your dog will jump over when you send him from a distance.

Next, try jumps with various objects decorating the sides of them. You'll find these decorations in competition, and your dog must get used to performing even when his vision of you is blocked.

When you start to practice the bar jump you may notice that your dog runs under it. A tarp taped below the jump can be useful to discourage this. Work one bar at a time, always going from the lowest to the highest.

When you're working on the long jump use the same methods, gradually spreading and increasing the hurdles to regulation width.

Sarah Says
If your dog is hesitant to jump over a hurdle, some treats in an empty yogurt container tossed over in front of him make a great lure.

Grrr
Once your dog is jumping the regulation height and distance, do not increase or decrease them. It will only confuse your dog.

Weave Poles

Weave poles are just what they sound like: poles your dog must weave through.

Some consider weave poles the most difficult obstacle to master. When I did Agility with my sweet Kyia, she liked them the most. Every dog is different.

A good command to use for the poles is Weave or Poles. Original, I know, but easy to remember.

Weave poles

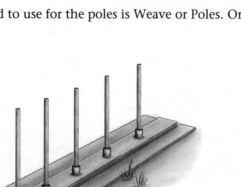

Sarah Says
Keep a short leash on your dog when practicing this obstacle. A long leash interferes, but a short leash allows you to guide if necessary.

Sarah Says
I'll betcha that your dog doesn't know his left from his right. If I'm right, it's time to teach him. Go back to Chapter 7.

Always start your dog to the right of the first pole. Stand on the right side of the poles and use encouragement that excites your dog as you guide him in and out.

At first, set a small goal (such as doing three poles correctly) and reward that. Increase as quickly as you both can to the regulation number. If need be, get into the training process yourself by weaving in and out like a snake. Come on now and put those hips into it!

Once your dog is catching on, work at greater distances from the poles. But don't be afraid to step back if your dog loses his concentration.

Pause Obstacles

These require your dog to pause for five seconds in the middle of running a course. Good luck!

➤ Pause table

➤ Pause box

Pause table and Pause box

Pause table. If it's your first time asking your dog to jump on a table, he may be utterly confused. He's probably thinking, "Aren't you always yelling at me for getting up here?" Start with a low table, encourage your dog with food or toys if necessary, and command "Table."

Once your dog is comfortable up there, give the command "Down." Help him if he doesn't get it at first. In competition your dog must stay still for five seconds, although waiting seven to ten seconds during practice won't hurt you any.

Progressively command your dog from greater distances until you are confident giving the command at twenty feet. And, as Jane Simmons-Moake points out, if you're planning on competing don't forget to practice on a damp table.

Pause box. Regulation style boxes are four feet square. Initially walk your dog to the box and explore it together. Use the command Box and help your dog jump into the box. When he's comfortable and understands the Box command, tell him Down (one time only!) and Stay. If your dog's feet poke out of the box, start again; he must stay in the box.

Regulations require the same five seconds. Practice until you are comfortable commanding from twenty feet away.

Tire Jump

This is just what it sounds like: A tire is suspended from a frame, and the dog jumps through it. Just like a tiger in the circus!

Begin by lowering the tire so that your dog can walk through it. Explore it together, then place your dog's leash through the opening. Have a helper encourage him through while you command "Tire" from behind or to the side.

Slowly pick up your pace, and raise the height. If your dog dashes under, tape a tarp under the tire to discourage this habit.

Grrr
Once you've progressed to regulation height, don't fiddle with the tire. You may cause a head-on collision, as your dog will miscalculate the height.

Official Stuff

You started Agility as a pastime, a hobby. But then you went to a competition or two, and now you're hooked. Not an unfamiliar story. If you feel your competitive juices flowing, there are many different classes of competition.

Standard Classes

These are the classes beginner dogs start out in. Each course is set up with eleven or twelve obstacles, and you and your dog race against the clock to finish. It's fun because you earn titles. (I love titles!) And once your dog completes the title you get to add initials to his name, just as if you had a doctor in the family.

➤ **Agility Dog (AD).** To get this title you have to perform one (just one!) flawless round in a Starters or Novice class.

➤ **Advanced Agility Dog (AAD).** You get this one after three flawless performances under two different judges in the Advanced class.

➤ **Master Agility Dog (MD).** This prestigious title is awarded to the dog who's had a flawless run in a Master class and qualified in a Gamblers class, a Pairs or Team class, a non-standard class, and one more, either non-standard or Masters run.

Non-Standard (Novelty) Classes

Once you get some experience you'll want to try your luck at some of the more unusual stuff. These classes have fun names. Go ahead and try them!

➤ **Gamblers.** Read closely. You can enter this class anywhere along your competition journey. The obstacles are laid out randomly and you get a set amount of time, so part of the fun is to see how many you can complete before the clock runs out. You get a higher score for contact equipment, less for hurdles. After the whistle blows you can quit or go to the gamblers corner. Here there are a fixed number of obstacles set up. If you send your dog and he's flawless, you get bonus points. If he messes up you get points taken off your previous score. Whatcha gonna do? It's a gamble.

➤ **Jumpers.** The only obstacles in this course are—you guessed it—jumps. Dogs love this one!

➤ **Snookers.** This is one high-energy class, and although the rules are a bit on the confusing side, I'm told once you try it you're hooked. In the opening sequence you complete three hurdles, alternating with three obstacles of your choice. Next comes the closing sequence of seven hurdles ranging in point values. The scores are given based on the number of points earned within a set time.

➤ **Pairs Relay.** This race is run with batons, just like in the Olympics. One dog completes the course, then passes off the baton to his partner. Scores are for the whole team.

➤ **Team.** Teams of four or more dogs run. At the end, all the scores and faults are tallied and the winner is the team with the best time score and the fewest faults.

Bet You Didn't Know

Each class will be given a Standard Course Time (SCT), which is determined by the length, in yards, of the course. Faults are added if you exceed the time limit or your dog refuses to perform, goes in the wrong direction, improperly performs an obstacle, or bumps a hurdle.

Competition Day

So you're off to the great contest. Good luck! Here are just a few tips before you go.

➤ Take water and food if it's an all-day event.

➤ Don't forget your dog's toys and treats. Sharing (your food) is okay, but if your dog has a favorite treat, bring it.

➤ Pack poop bags. Your fellow competitors will appreciate your consideration.

➤ Check your dog's nails for clipping and coat for parasites. Dogs don't perform as well when they're uncomfortable.

Sarah Says
Before you go, consider the weather conditions—as you leave and later in the day. Are you expecting it to get cooler? If so you might want to pack a sweater, for you and your dog. Going someplace warmer? Bring some cooling off gear for the hot weather.

Once you get to the show grounds, introduce your dog to the obstacles. Although the course will not be completely set up, you can walk your dog about and get him in the right frame of mind. Pay special attention to all contact zones, reminding your dog that touching them is a necessary evil wherever you go. If he has an accident tell the steward.

You'll be able to walk through the course alone once it is set up. In her book *Agility Training,* Jane Simmons-Moake recommends that you go through the motions, watching out for anything unusual that might confuse your dog.

A warm-up is also essential, as the course requires a fair amount of athleticism. But don't turn your warm-up into a workout. Tiring your dog out before the competition is not the best idea.

When you get to the starting line everyone's nerves are going to be on edge. Staying calm will keep your dog calm. The rule is that all clocks start the second your dog crosses the starting line, so make sure you're both on the same wavelength. Once you're out of the gate, you're not allowed to touch your dog, so your commands and steadiness will be his only guide. And whether yours was a good or bad performance, praise that dog!

To get more information on competition rules or to find clubs in your area, you can write to:

The American Kennel Club (AKC)
5580 Centerview Dr.
Raleigh, NC 27606
(919) 233-9767

United States Dog Agility Association (USDAA)
P.O. Box 850955
Richardson, TX 75085
(214) 231-9700

National Club for Dog Agility (NCDA)
401 Bluemont Circle
Manhattan, KS 66502
(913) 537-7022

Sarah Says
If my brief description leaves you thirsty for more, go out and buy a book on Agility. There are more and more on the market. I find Jane Simmons-Moake's book, *Agility Training, The Fun Sport for All Dogs*, to be very informative. In addition to all the ins and out, she goes over how to construct or where to buy obstacles.

Whether you do it for recreation or competition, Agility is fun for everybody. And what a great way to tire your dog out.

The Least You Need to Know

➤ A sport for all dogs of all sizes, Agility tests a dog's ability to maneuver over and through equipment, and the human handler's ability to guide their dog along a specified route. It's a great way to get out with other dog-loving people and have fun with your dog.

➤ When you're starting out in Agility, it's always best to start with classes given by an organized club.

➤ Let your dog sniff, examine, and explore each obstacle before you attempt to teach him how to negotiate it.

➤ To start, simplify each obstacle by lowering or shortening it. Gradually build up the difficulty.

➤ Praise your dog warmly and lovingly every step of the way.

Track and Field

Got a dog whose instincts won't give her a rest? Consider a sporting event designed to fit your dog's natural ability. The American Kennel Club sponsors many breed-specific competitive events celebrating the capabilities of purebred dogs. For example, the herding trials recognize the breeds bred to move flocks and herds, lure coursing honors sighthounds and earthdog trials put the tenacity of the terrier group to the test.

If you've got a mixed breed that would love to herd, hunt or go to ground (terrier-type lingo for earthdog), don't despair! Although the AKC only allows purebreds in its competitions, many local clubs and training groups welcome all comers.

AKC Obedience Trials

Here's an interesting piece of trivia. The very first Obedience competition in the United States was held in 1933 in a town right near where I live: Mount Kisco, New York. Until then, dog shows focused exclusively on the dog's conformation or, in layman's terms, his looks.

Obedience trials don't take a dog's physical appearance into account at all. Although dogs must be purebreds to enter this ring, the only thing that wins brownie points is good temperament and mindful behavior.

Competition in the Obedience ring is divided into three levels, each more difficult than the previous one. At each level a competitor is working for an AKC Obedience title.

➤ Novice - Companion Dog (CD)

➤ Open - Companion Dog Excellent (CDX)

➤ Utility - Utility Dog (UD)

To receive an Obedience title, a dog must earn three "legs" in competition. To achieve a "leg" a dog must score at least one hundred seventy points out of a possible two hundred and get more than half the points available for each exercise. The exercises vary for each class.

There are also two more titles. Utility Dog Excellent (UDX) is earned by qualifying in both the Utility and Open classes at ten shows. Utility Dogs that are ranked first or second in Open B or Utility classes can earn points toward an Obedience Trial Champion (OTCh) title. (B classes are for experienced handlers, while A classes are for beginners whose dogs have never received a title.)

Bet You Didn't Know

Although mixed breeds can't take part in AKC competitions, they have their own activity club with similar rules and certifications. To find out more, contact the nearest SPCA or humane society, or write:

Mixed Breed Dog Club of America
Phyllis Massa
1937 Seven Pines Dr.
St. Louis, MO 63146-3717

Each class requires the dog to have different skills, In the Novice class, a dog must heel on leash, stand to be examined by a judge, heel off leash, recall (Come), and do a group long sit and long down. In the Open class a dog must heel off leash, drop on recall, retrieve on a flat surface, retrieve over the high jump, broad jump, long sit and long down. In the Utility class a dog must respond to a signal exercise, pass two scent discrimination tests, perform a directed retrieve, perform directed jumping, and stand for a group examination.

These are all formal exercises with very specific rules, and training for them is beyond the scope of this book. However, there are many Obedience clubs throughout the country and also many excellent books and videos that can help you. You'll find some of them listed in the Appendix.

If you've got a well-mannered, obedient dog resting nearby and your eyes are lighting up at the thought of a little friendly competition, this might be just the challenge for you both!

Earthdog

Do you have a terrier whose digging instincts are driving you crazy? If so, these trials might be the perfect outlet for him. Terriers, you see, were originally bred to go to ground; that means to chase vermin all the way into their underground burrows, and bring them back dead or alive.

The breeds allowed to compete include all the small terriers in the Terrier Group, as well as Dachshunds. Toy breeds are not allowed to compete in official AKC events, although some, such as the Yorkshire Terrier, are certainly terriers and may enjoy themselves at a fun match.

At the test site a series of tunnels (called the den) is set up with a caged rodent at the end. The dog enters the tunnel at one end, finds the rodent at the other, and barks. (In these tests, the rodent emerges still caged and still alive.)

Tests are run at four different levels. In Introduction to Quarry the dog does not receive any qualifications or titles, but simply gets a taste of what it's like to be in a den and scent the prey. After passing this test, dogs advance gradually through the ranks. Titles are awarded for Junior Earthdog (JE), Senior Earthdog (SE), and Master Earthdog (ME). Each test requires a

Sarah Says
While earthdog tests might seem as if the dogs get back to nature and let their instincts run wild, in fact dogs must be under their handler's control at all times, even when they're under ground. Recall and other requirements test the training of even the toughest terrier.

greater degree of skill in detecting and following a scent, and in gameness and den savvy than the previous one. The distances from which a dog must locate the den, and the complexity of the tunnels it must maneuver in the dark, become increasingly more difficult.

Participation in AKC Events

Sport	Number of Events	Number of Dogs
Agility	253	28,651
Earthdog	47	3,218
Field Trials	1,416	137,432
Herding	226	3,711
Hunting Tests	809	38,501
Lure Coursing	395	6,380
Obedience	2,214	103,787
Tracking	271	1,297

All figures supplied by the American Kennel Club for official events in 1996.

Herding Tests and Trials

Many farmers and ranchers throughout the world still use herding dogs to control their livestock. Many dogs in the Herding Group, who are living their lives as cherished pets, still take their herding genes very seriously. You'd notice them in a minute: They're the ones herding their owners from the kitchen, rounding up the school children as they get off the bus, and staring fixedly as the Discovery Channel airs a special called *Sheep of the Scottish Highlands.*

Herding dogs come in different types. Shepherds work in front of livestock, usually sheep, and use an intense gaze, known as "the eye" to control their herd. The Border Collie and Bearded Collie are two shepherd breeds.

Drovers work behind sheep or cattle herds and drive them forward. They sometimes control the animals by nipping at their heels. Both the Pembroke and Cardigan Welsh Corgis fall into this category, as does the Australian Cattle Dog.

Livestock Guards do just that; they don't move the flock, they guard it. Bred to work independently, they are raised with the flock and are expected to guard it from wolves, bears, and thieves. These are all big dogs, and include the Kuvasz, Komondor, and Great Pyrenees.

All Around Farm Dogs are bred to stay around the farm responding minute-to-minute to any task that comes up. The Collie, German Shepherd, and Australian Shepherd are in this group.

Training a herding dog does not have to start in puppyhood. Although many instincts are noticeable in a young dog, some don't show any talent until they're older. If you are interested in pursuing this activity, it's important to remember that you are encouraging your dog's instinct to herd or guard, not to chase or kill. When the first herding dog was bred from the wolf, the prey instincts were suppressed. Rough handling or tugging games can spoil a good herding dog.

> **Sarah Says**
> During training, let your dog be your guide. Every dog is unique and to teach a good herder to work with you, you must learn how to expose their natural abilities.

To the Hunt

If you're a hunting enthusiast and you've got a dog that likes to tag along, these events might be for you. There are almost as many kinds of hunting and field trials as there are dogs, and the AKC is only one of many organizations that sponsors them. But all have one thing in common: They put hunter and dog back together at a task the dog was originally bred to do.

Hounds are traditionally tested in their pursuit of prey. Beagles and the Basset Hounds work in packs and are judged by how well they work together and follow a trail. Dachshunds work in pairs (called a brace) and are judged on their ability to run a rabbit into the ground. There are also Coonhound trials sponsored by the AKC and other groups.

Pointing Dogs were originally bred to search fields far ahead of their owners and stop and point if they found a bird. Trials are often run with the hunter on horseback following the hunting dog. A dog on point is a beautiful thing to see.

Retrievers retrieve shot game. In these trials a hunter may shoot one or several birds, and the dog may be required to swim to the birds or even retrieve them from the water.

> **Sarah Says**
> The best way to find out about hunting tests in your area is to hang out with the hunters. Ask at your local field and hunting supply store, check the bulletin board where you go for your state hunting license—you get the idea.

This young Labrador Retriever knows what to do with a downed duck.

Spaniels were bred to hunt close to man and flush out birds within gunshot range. They are also expected to retrieve the game once it is shot.

Lure Coursing

The sport of Lure Coursing was set up in 1972 by the American Sighthound Association. Its goal is to "preserve and further develop the natural beauty, grace, speed, and coursing skill of the Sighthound." All the sighthounds may take part in Lure Coursing events, including Afghan Hounds, Borzoi, Greyhounds, Ibizan Hounds, Irish Wolfhounds, Pharaoh Hounds, Salukis, Scottish Deerhounds, and Whippets. These dogs all have one thing in common: They love to run after game very fast!

Modern Lure Coursing uses no game. Instead, an artificial lure is pulled along a 1,000- to 1,500-yard course that zigs and zags to the test the dog's speed, agility, skill, enthusiasm, and endurance.

As anyone who has witnessed a competition can tell you, sighthounds respond to a lure on pure instinct. They do what they were bred for, which is to chase a moving object.

Sighthounds aren't the only breeds that love to run, of course, and many clubs hold fun matches where any breed can enter. If your dog loves to chase, this may be the best way to redirect his energies.

Bet You Didn't Know

One of the key players in a Lure Coursing event is the lure operator. His job is to keep the lure ten to thirty yards in front of the lead dog, make sure it never gets tangled, and stop it within twenty yards of the lure machine.

Hot on the Trail

Dog's noses are analogous to our eyes. Tracking to them is like looking around to us. However, to train your dog to follow a specific trail is no simple feat. Tracking is advanced work and requires a lot of encouragement and patient repetition.

You can use tracking as a recreational sport, teaching your dog to find various people or objects in your family, or you can use it as a competitive sport, earning tracking titles. Consider teaching basic tracking for personal convenience! Having a helper to round up the troops for dinner, or find a child who's wandered off can be a tremendous asset!

Tracking skills can also be used with a search and rescue group. Tracking dogs have been used by the police and individuals to find lost people when all other efforts have failed.

Sarah Says
Exposing a dog to different weather conditions and locations is important in creating a reliable tracking dog.

Training must start with good communication. Positive retrieves, where the article is within sight, is the best place to start. As a dog's ability and enthusiasm increase, articles can be hidden from sight in tall grass or around corners.

The American Kennel Club offers two kinds of tracking competitions: field and variable surface. Variable surface tracking goes across roads, parking lots, and other urban areas, while field tracking is strictly in the wild. Titles are Tracking Dog (TD) and Tracking Dog Excellent (TDX), and Variable Surface Tracker (VST) and Champion Tracker (CT).

Breed-Specific Working Titles

Many national breed clubs have designated individual working titles to test for the abilities their breed was first developed to possess. For example, the Newfoundland Club of America sponsors clinics and competitions where dogs can earn Water Dog (WD) and Water Rescue Dog (WRD) titles. They also award the drafting titles Draft Dog (DD) and Team Draft Dog (TDD).

Many other breed clubs also sponsor events. The Dalmatian Club of America offers road titles. The Alaskan Malamute offers titles for weight pulls. And there's lots more. To discover what your breed club has to offer, write your national club (you can get a list of national breed clubs from the AKC).

Contact Listings

American Kennel Club
5580 Centerview Drive
Raleigh, NC 27606-3390

American Sighthound Field Association
P.O. Box 1293-M
Woodstock, GA 30188

American Herding Breed Association
Linda Rorem
1548 Victoria Way
Pacifica, CA 94044

Earth Dog Trials
Patricia Adams/Entry Trial Secretary
Dogwood Cottage RD2
Box 38A
Franklinton, NC 27525

Livestock Guarding Dog Project
Livestock Guard Dog Association
Hampshire College
P.O. Box FC
Amherst, MA 01002

United Kennel Club
100 E. Kilgore Road
Kalamazoo, MI 49001-5593

The Least You Need to Know

➤ Sometimes the best way to deal with your dog's natural instincts is to engage him in healthy competition.

➤ Earning a title is a great honor, but it's only a small piece of the pie. Working with your dog should be your number one incentive, whether or not you're ever recognized.

➤ The best way to get involved in organized competition is to seek out a club of like-minded enthusiasts in your area. The AKC can send you a list of local clubs.

➤ Advanced training cannot be learned from a book. Though reading helps, it cannot replace experience.

Discus Dog

If you've ever played Frisbee and noticed your dog eyeing the disc eagerly (and who hasn't?), this could be the sporting event for you. According to Peter Bloeme, the author of *Frisbee Dogs,* there are already 300,000 dog-human Frisbee partnerships that compete across the United States. Whether or not you're part of this population, I promise you one thing: Once you've seen a sponsored Frisbee Dog event, you'll never look at your disc, your dog, or your tossing technique the same way again.

Illegal Origins

If you were a Dodger fan in August of 1974, you played a part in this story. If not, you'll get a kick out of it anyway. During a game a fan named Alex Stein broke onto the field and for eight minutes dazzled the fans with his dog Ashley Whippet (a Whippet, of course) and a Frisbee.

Unfortunately, despite his great performance Alex was arrested and Ashley disappeared for a few heart-wrenching days. Fortunately, the two were reunited and gained nationwide attention, appearing on television shows such as *The Today Show, Good Morning America, The Late Show With David Letterman* and *The Tonight Show*. Not a bad schedule for a law breaker and his sidekick!

Alex and Ashley set out to gain recognition for their sport, and they succeeded. Other people involved in the sport had a rallying point and were brought together for the first time: Alex Stein, Irv Lander, Eldon McIntire and his Australian Shepherd Hyper Hank became the founding fathers of canine Frisbee.

The first official canine contests were tied in with the World Frisbee Championship at the Rose Bowl, but within a short time individual contests and exhibitions were being set up across the country. Now canine Frisbee contests are sponsored by national companies. Quite a way to come just twenty years after that fateful August day!

Bet You Didn't Know

Flying discs are an American invention. In 1871 a Bridgeport, Connecticut, resident named William Russell Frisbie took over a bakery and renamed it *The Frisbie Pie Company*. At its peak the place was turning out 80,000 pies a day. Not a bad way to make a living! Life went on this way pretty unremarkably until August 25, 1957, when *The New York Times* noted, in a story on the company's pie plates, "It's common knowledge in New Haven that Frisbie … is a way of life." The rest, as they say, is history.

Disc Basics

This section isn't for your dog, dear readers, it's for you. If you can't toss the Frisbee predictably, your dog will give up on you. So find yourself a good nine and a quarter-inch diameter disc, prop this book open, and let's start with lesson number one.

The Grip

Place your thumb on the outside edge and curl your fingers under the lip. Don't white-knuckle the thing. A firm grasp will do. Carry it around the house for a couple of days. Now you're talking.

The Stance

With your feet shoulder width apart, point the shoulder of your tossing arm at the object you're aiming for. Although you'll end up shifting your weight forward, you should always keep some weight on each foot.

The Toss

The toss must be smooth and sharp and even. A thrust back with your elbow and a snap of your wrist will project the disc forward. Make sure your shoulder stays aligned with your target, your head is up, and your eyes are looking out ahead of you.

Of course, this isn't the only way to toss a Frisbee, but it's a start. Once you're totally accurate in your toss, go out without your dog and play around with your grip. Get a true Frisbee guide, or read Peter Bloeme's *Frisbee Dogs*. These books will illustrate how the professionals toss and take you through a number of toss styles step by step.

> **Sarah Says**
> Flying discs need care too. Dishwashers are great for keeping them clean and free from slobber. A fine sandpaper will keep your disc free of dangerous edges, though once your disc is demolished, you'll have to say good-bye. The greatest expense in having a Frisbee dog is not the dog, it's the Frisbees.

Training for the Fly

You can start puppies at two or three months, but don't push them. If you've got an older dog at your feet, you're not too late. As long as your dog's stimulated by a flying disc, any age will do. Pups should not be asked to jump until their growth plates are formed, at about one year of age. Of course, all dogs must know basic obedience skills to move on to anything more complicated, including Frisbee games, but I'll leave that up to you.

> **Bet You Didn't Know**
> I was shocked to discover how many types of Frisbees there are on the market. The Wham-O company had the patent for a long time (and the Frisbee name is still trademarked), but once the patent expired manufacturers flooded the market. There's a disc with a thumb pad, ones with bones on the top, small ones, donut ones, and fabric ones. The best for your purposes is either a fabric or a hard plastic disc. Pups can start with a three-inch diameter disc and grow up to the regulation size.

According to Peter Bloeme, who is also a Frisbee dog champion, you should follow this basic format when training your dog to a disc.

First, treat the disc as a dinner plate. It looks like one anyway, right? For a week feed your dog on the disc, picking it up after each meal to prevent chewing. Wash and hide the disc until the next feeding.

Grrr
Do not spin your dog around like an airplane when he's got a grip on the Frisbee. Rough tug-of-war matches encourage behavior you don't really want to see in any dog.

Practice inside initially. Tease your dog playfully with the disc, saying "Get It." When he grabs it, tug *lightly* to ensure a secure grip before you get him to release it by offering food or tremendous praise.

Now play keep away. Show your dog the disc and run a short distance before allowing him to grasp it. To see if your dog is sufficiently in love with this new object, turn it upside down and slide it a short distance away from you on the floor. When your dog grasps it, praise him tremendously.

Start by simply showing your dog the disc and helping him learn to love it.

Initially your dog probably won't want to give the disc back to you. That's okay; worry about the good retrieving skills after you've nailed the grab.

Try the keep-away game with a new disc that hasn't been used as a dinner plate. Your dog might react totally different. Keep the praise high every time he grasps the disc.

Are you sure he loves it, now? It's time to teach the return.

➤ Place a ten-foot light lead or rope on your dog during an otherwise fun Frisbee time.

➤ When he grabs the disc encourage him to come back. If he returns with or without the disc, praise him wildly. If he decides not to, snap the lead and reel him in. Again, you're concentrating on the return, with or without the disc.

➤ After your dog is cooperating, try it off-leash, although if you practice outside stay within an enclosure.

➤ Next, practice with five or six discs, encouraging your dog to return to you before you toss the next one.

➤ If your dog doesn't start bringing the discs back to you, you'll need to practice in a small room or fenced enclosure. Toss or roll the disc on the ground.

➤ If he looks up at you disc-less, encourage him with Get It.

➤ If he still refuses, ignore him. He'll probably start hitting you with the disc to get you to play. Yes! Good dog!

Now you're ready to take your lessons outside. Make or buy a thirty-foot line and knot the end for easy handling. Progress through your early lessons quickly to remind your dog that he's expected to do the same thing outside that you taught him inside. If he decides to make a break for it, step securely on the end of the line. Don't correct him; he'll do the math when he hits the end. Stop the lesson and ignore him for an hour.

Start with short tosses to make sure your dog gets the hang of catching the disc.

Day-to-day lessons should start with short tosses and progress to the tough stuff. Remember, dogs are like us—they need to get warmed up.

Bet You Didn't Know

Disc colors can help or hurt your dog. Dark discs on a dark day are hard to track. White is better. White on a bright or cloudy day, however, can be hard to make out. Yellow or red is best for a sunny day.

All this and we still haven't covered the art of catching. Your dog should be fielding grounders and rollers only. To teach the catch, I'll defer to expert Peter Bloeme again.

➤ Bring your dog to the bursting level with disc excitement. Tease, tug, roll—whatever charges him up.

Sarah Says
Always allow your dog to watch the disc. You can have him stand at different angles to you, right next to you or in front of you, but don't block his view of the disc.

➤ Kneel down and lightly toss the disc at your dog's nose. If he misses the catch, pick it up. Only let him have the disc if he catches it. His days of grabbing the disc off the ground are over.

➤ Your dog may get frustrated, but keep it up until he starts to grab the disc in the air.

➤ Now practice with several discs tossed out three feet. Slowly shorten the time between each toss.

➤ After he's got the quick toss, slow it down again tossing the disc to your left. When the left is good, go right.

To tie in the catching with the running and tossing, begin by holding the disc above your dog's head as you tell him Get It. Make sure you *always* hold the disc parallel to the ground, the way the dog will see it on the fly. When your dog grabs on tight, let go. Remember, if your dog drops the disc, pick it up silently and start again. No more grounders.

Now a short toss here and one over there. Progress slowly, don't be afraid to go back a step or two, and remember the two W's: water and warm-up.

Stop rewarding grounders after your dog really has the hang of it.

The Competitive Edge

Getting good? Want to test your skills in front of a crowd? Go for it!

Competitions are usually held at different levels. Community affairs are a less serious gathering, but lots of fun. The home crowd is always the most supportive, too. For true competition, however, you'll need to go to the Regional or Open level. Dogs winning at the Open level qualify for World Finals, which are held at the Washington Monument in Washington D.C. Too cool!

The first thing you'll need to do is write for contest info:

> Canine Frisbee Championships
> 4060 D-Peachtree Road
> Suite 326
> Atlanta, GA 30319
> (800) 786-9240

Grrr
The most common Frisbee dog injuries are not sprained limbs or broken legs. They're dehydration and mouth injuries. Many dogs bite their tongue reaching for the disc or cut their mouth on a cracked edge. And again, I can't stress enough the importance of always offering fresh water.

In competition there are two rounds: the mini distance and the free flight. In the mini distance round you're given one disc and sixty seconds, and are scored on the number of complete throws. Points are also awarded for three-pawed (in the air) and two-pawed catches.

The free flight round is a more choreographed performance. Each team is given sixty seconds in community competitions or ninety seconds in Regional or Open finals to strut their stuff. Scores are awarded based on the difficulty and the originality of the material. Music makes this routine more fun for the audience and encourages more participation than the mini distance event.

Sarah Says
The day of the competition, pack your dog's bag with food and water, familiar bowls, toys and treats, proof of vaccines, bags to clean up poop, and some snacks for yourself.

Female dogs in heat can't compete, and overtly aggressive behavior or abuse of a dog disqualify a team. Hard to believe anybody could abuse their dog, isn't it?

In *Frisbee Dogs*, Peter Bloeme recommends from personal experience that appearance, for both you and your dog, really makes a difference. Dress for the weather and coordinate with your dog. For example, red shows up a black dog well; tie a red bandanna around your dog's neck and you'll be the envy of everyone.

The Least You Need to Know

➤ Practice throwing the Frisbee by yourself first. Your dog can't catch it if you can't throw it reasonably well.

➤ Once your dog gets interested in the disc, only let him have it if he catches it.

➤ Dehydration is a real danger when playing canine Frisbee. Keep plenty of water on hand for both of you.

➤ Be sure to keep your disc clean and smooth. Dirty or damaged discs can be dangerous for your dog.

Chapter 20

Four-Footed Flyball

In This Chapter

➤ What is Flyball?

➤ Learning the ropes

➤ Equipment and set-ups

➤ Clubs and competition

This game is quite unlike anything else in the dog world. To play Flyball you need a team of at least four spirited dogs with a slight obsession for tennis balls. Sound like someone in your home? Other advantages are a penchant for running, jumping, and coming when called. Coming when called? Yes! This is one sport that can actually improve your dog's reaction to the Come command.

What Is It?

That was the first question I asked, too. From the brief description it sounded like a free-for-all with balls and dogs and hurdles. However, the person I asked assured me, "I know there are rules; it's a recognized sport." So I looked into it. This is what I discovered: Flyball is a sport that organizes a dog's love of running, retrieving, and catching balls into a team competition the whole family can be a part of.

Flyball is a team sport for dogs that was invented in California in the late 1970s. Legend has it that Herbert Wagner first showed it to millions of Americans on *The Tonight Show*. Soon afterward dog trainers and dog clubs were making and using Flyball boxes.

In the early 1980s the sport became so popular that the North American Flyball Association (NAFA) was formed. It is now the worldwide authority for Flyball.

Roughly, here's how the game is played: Two teams of four dogs each race against each other and the clock. Each dog runs one length of the course, which consists of jumping over four hurdles to a ball box, pressing a lever on the box to release the ball, catching the ball, and racing with it back over the hurdles to the starting point. The team that finishes with the fastest time and the fewest faults wins the heat. The race winner is the team that wins the best two out of three heats or three out of five.

Flyball Lingo

Of course, it gets a little more complicated than that. There is some Flyball terminology I'll need to introduce you to.

Teams. Each team can include as many as six dogs and as few as four. Flyball is open to all dogs of pure or mixed heritage that are at least one year old. Though only four dogs are permitted to compete in each heat, they may be interchanged due to strategy or injury, and the jumps adjusted accordingly.

Jumps. The jumps are set four inches below the withers (shoulder) of the smallest dog running. Eight inches is the minimum height and sixteen inches is the maximum height. The jumps may be changed from heat to heat.

Bet You Didn't Know

Which breeds do best in Flyball? Herding and retrieving breeds predominate at competitions. Some think small dogs would slow down a team. *Au contrare*—they are often the heroes. Since the jumps are adjusted to the height of the smallest dog on the team, their presence improves overall time scores.

Passing. This is the relay part. Rather than a starter pistol, Flyball competitions use lights to indicate the equivalent of "On your mark, get set, go!" The dogs are actually released from a distance behind the starting line, so they are at full speed when they cross the line. As the first dog returns, the second dog is also released from behind the line, so that as the first dog crosses the line coming in, the second dog is crossing the line going out.

And so on. The point is that the release must occur at the same time as the return. In a perfect world it would work every time, but it's not a perfect world.

Faults. Early passes, missed jumps, and dropped balls receive faults. Depending on the severity or number of faults, dogs must run again. Though it would seem disastrous, often both teams collect enough faults to warrant a second run-through. Funny, but the dogs don't seem to mind!

The Course

Does it still seem a bit foggy? It's quite an adventure, I promise you that. Let's take a look at the course. Although your interest doesn't have to extend to competition, I'll take you through a regulation set-up.

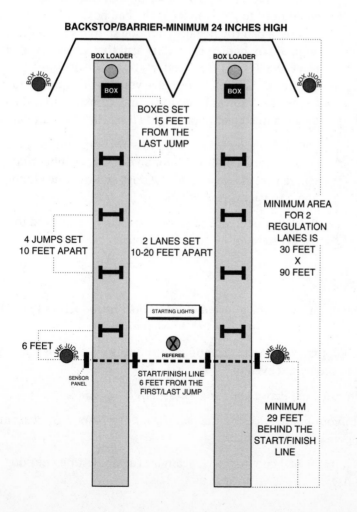

BACKSTOP/BARRIER-MINIMUM 24 INCHES HIGH

BOX JUDGE

BOX LOADER

BOX

BOX LOADER

BOX

BOX JUDGE

BOXES SET 15 FEET FROM THE LAST JUMP

MINIMUM AREA FOR 2 REGULATION LANES IS 30 FEET X 90 FEET

4 JUMPS SET 10 FEET APART

2 LANES SET 10-20 FEET APART

STARTING LIGHTS

6 FEET

LINE JUDGE

REFEREE

LINE JUDGE

SENSOR PANEL

START/FINISH LINE 6 FEET FROM THE FIRST/LAST JUMP

MINIMUM 29 FEET BEHIND THE START/FINISH LINE

A typical Flyball course

The entire course is thirty to ninety feet long, and two lanes are set up ten to twenty feet apart. When held indoors, mats are placed to ensure secure footing. Each set of jumps is placed four feet apart; the first is six feet from the start/finish line and the last is fifteen feet from the ball box. There is a twenty-nine-foot passing area in front of the start/finish line, and a twenty-four-inch barrier beyond the ball box to stop any over-enthusiastic competitors.

Sarah Says
Mastering the code of the safety lights is a true accomplishment. Amber, amber, green flashed at one-second intervals means "On your mark, get set, go!" The top red light indicates when the dogs cross the starting light. A blinking bottom red light indicates a false start.

And no course is complete without its fair share of electricity. Sensor panels are placed at the start line to detect early passes and safety lights are displayed to indicate any activity of the sensor panel and to start the race.

If you'd like to set up a course of your own, the first thing you'll need to get or make is the ball box. This contraption releases a ball the instant your dog steps on the lever. The original box had an extending arm that gave a few dogs a black eye. Poor things! Today's boxes are designed to release the ball safely and give your dog the proper footing to turn back toward the finish line. Constructing a box is detailed in a great book called *Flying High* by Joan Payne.

Sarah Says
In her book *Flying High*, Joan Payne recommends raiding the tennis ball graveyard at a local court or club. A club of enthusiastic Flyball dogs can run through many, many balls in just a few practices!

Tennis balls are usually the balls of choice, but this can be tricky—not all balls work for all dogs. Remember that you're part of a team and the dogs and their needs are going to vary. It's inevitable.

But let's not create a problem yet. First you'll need to concentrate on just one dog: yours.

Training for Flyball

The rest of your dog's Flyball career will be affected by his proper introduction to the ball box. Just like any other kind of training, this is a step-by-step process.

➤ Show your dog the box first, with no expectations or training commands. Place a treat on top of the box to be discovered.

➤ Roll a ball down into the box. Praise your dog if he grabs it.

➤ Now hide the ball in your hand, releasing the ball if your dog paws it. Start saying "Paw" when his response becomes a habit.

➤ Placing ball after ball in the ball cup, trigger it again and again, letting your dog explore the situation.

➤ Next, load the box and let your dog investigate it. Ecstatically encourage any pawing interest. If your dog presses too lightly, trigger the ball for him. If your dog gets hit in the face or is spooked, adjust the cup hand so it releases at a different angle and go back a few steps.

Jumping hurdles is something most dogs love to do, once they get the hang of it.

Once your dog puts it together, it's time to teach him how to run the course. This can get pretty compli-cated, and you will be training with a team, anyway, so chances are you'll all go through the set-ups with help from a veteran. But there are some important training concepts you need to remember.

➤ The first time you send your dog, ask a training partner to stand at the box and direct your dog in. Start from four feet away and progress to twenty feet, using the command Hit It.

➤ Encourage the retrieval, initially by running from your dog as he turns toward you with the ball.

➤ Set the first *low* jump six feet to eight feet from the box.

Sarah Says
If your dog's a food hound or a dinner gobbler you can start teaching the straight-on approach ahead of time. Have someone put the food or treat atop the box, twenty feet away, while your dog watches. Pump your dog up with, "What is it? Is that for you? Looks good, huh?" When he's about to burst, release him with the command Hit It.

➤ Run the course the first few times with your dog and run back to your starting point as he runs forward to the box.

Grrr
Flyball doesn't include the word or the concept "No." Redirect your dog's behavior, but don't scold.

➤ Slowly pull the jump back until your dog perfects the routine at fifteen feet. This might take a while, so be patient.

➤ Gates along the side of the course to keep your dog on track are a real help as you introduce more hurdles.

➤ Once your dog will run the regulation course, introduce a second lane with another dog to prepare him for the distractions of competition.

Real Competition

When NAFA was founded in 1985 it started out with ten members of a single team. By 1995 the number grew to 290 regular teams, and 142 Multibreed teams. This is great for the sport, since the more entries in a competition, the more exciting for all involved.

Each team is divided into two classes: regular and non-regular. In the regular class the team may consist of four dogs from different backgrounds.

Non-regular classes include Peewee, Veterans, and Multibreed.

Multibreed is the largest in the registry. This class consists of four different purebred dogs and one mixed-breed dog.

The NAFA further divides the teams into divisions, which classify dogs based on similar time scores.

Besides the team winners, individual dogs are awarded points for clean heats (no faults), based on their team's times, whether or not they win. If a dog runs the course in thirty-two seconds, he gets one point; under twenty-eight seconds wins five points and under twenty-four seconds wins twenty-five points. What can you do with those points? Take a look at the table on the next page.

Bet You Didn't Know

Guess the record? A brief, faultless 16.96 seconds—which probably doesn't mean much until you've been to a competition. But once you have, you'll be amazed.

These cool initials you can put after to your dog's name are awarded based on the number of points acquired.

Titles

Flyball Dog	FD	20 points
Flyball DogExcellent	FDX	100 points
Flyball DogChampion	FDCh	500 points
Flyball Master	FM	5000 points
Flyball MasterExcellent	FMX	10,000 points
Flyball MasterChampion	FMCh	15,000 points
Flyball MasterGrand Champion	FGrCh	20,000 points

Imagine how many competitions you'd have to attend to acquire 20,000 points! It's mind boggling.

Before you send for your first competition application, send for the official rule book. To obtain a copy of the official rules or to inquire about teams in your area contact NAFA at:

> P.O. Box 8
> Mount Hope, Ontario
> L0R 1W0 Canada

Sarah Says
The Flyball Home Page is located at:

http://www.cs.umn.edu/~ianhogg/flyball/flyball.html

Rules are $10 U.S. and the other information is free.

The Least You Need to Know

➤ Dogs that love to retrieve and jump are going to love Flyball.

➤ Since Flyball requires a dog to run out and back, a solid recall is vital. Make sure your dog *knows* Come.

➤ Make sure your dog has plenty of time to learn about the Flyball box before you begin training him to run the course.

➤ Before you start, contact the NAFA and get the rule book and information about local clubs.

Winter Olympics

When most people think of dogs and snow, they think of a Husky-type with a thick coat and a curly tail. Snow sports and activities, however, are not limited by breed. When I was five I went to a local nature preserve to witness a sledding event and saw a team of two Standard Poodles draw up. Needless to say, they weren't sporting the usual show ring clip!

For all of you snow enthusiasts who have dogs that get a rush out of taking you for a walk, grab a pencil and read closely. Dogs and snow are a wonderful mix and, although I wouldn't encourage any Toy dog owners to go out in a blizzard, the activities in this chapter are not limited by breed.

Sledding

I loved snow as a kid; the only thing I loved more was my Husky dog, Shawbee. One of the greatest gifts I ever received was an official sled dog harness; finally, something we could really get into together!

If your dog is big enough and strong enough to pull you, he's got what it takes to start sledding. Of course, snow helps. If you don't have that, you can flip to the carting section in Chapter 22 and read up on that. This chapter is for snow lovers only!

First things first. You'll need equipment.

Harnesses

There are many versions, and you'd do best talking to an expert to determine what's best for you. You'll also need to find a distributor who knows how to read and translate your dog's measurements. Improperly fit, a harness can be painful and even dangerous.

Sarah Says
Just because the word "race" is in the name of the harnesses, it doesn't mean you have to. Sledding can be a purely recreational activity or something you can try first for fun and then compete when you are ready.

Typically you'll select from four options:

1. **Cross-back or Switch-back Racing Harness.** This one has a high comfort factor and distributes weight evenly from the dog to the sled.

2. **Light-weight Race Harness.** Same as above, minus the cross piece over the dog's back. This type of harness can be a pain if you're going for distance.

3. **Weight Pulling Harness.** Though similar to the racing harness, this has a lower center of gravity and a space bar that rests on the thighs.

4. **Freight Harness.** Same as a weight pull, but made from leather.

Sleds

Next you'll need to consider a sled. Dogs have a natural urge to pull kids around on a leash, so why not redirect this instinct? The sled makes it easier for the dog and more fun. Here are some choices:

1. **Light-weight Sprint Sleds.** These are designed for racing short distances and recreational sledding. This is what Shawbee and I grew up with.

2. **Toboggan Sleds.** These are used in sprint sledding and long distance events.

3. **Freight Sleds.** These are used for towing the heavy stuff.

Make sure you get just the right sled for your dog.

What's missing? You've got the sled. You've fit a good harness. Now you'll need something to attach the two. The piece that attaches the dog to the sled is called a gangline. A tugline is the piece that connects the harness to the ganglines and distributes the sled's weight evenly for maximum comfort. If you're looking into sledding or weight pulling as a serious hobby you'll want to invest in four safety lines as well, should the main snaps break.

The final thing you need to consider is your clothing. You can sweat profusely after running behind the sled for five minutes, even in subzero temperatures, but you must think smart and dress for all extremes. Rules of thumb: layer and avoid wool. The fabric of hats and gloves should be lightweight and waterproof. If it's windy, wear a face mask. Sunglasses are a must, even on a cloudy day. And remember, it's always better to overdress than underdress.

Now let's have a look at that dog of yours. What breed? Any large dog can pull a sled, but your dog's build will dictate the kind of pulling they most enjoy. Large boned, lumbering breeds can pull heavier weights more slowly over longer distances. Leggy breeds that are light on their feet can pull less, faster, over shorter distances. If you've got a long-coated or wire-coated breed, you'll need to trim their fur (especially around their feet) so snow doesn't build up in their coat.

Bet You Didn't Know

What's the latest fashion for sled dogs? Booties! Attractive and secure, many mushers use them to protect their dogs' feet.

As you can see so far, sledding is a complex activity requiring a fair bit of specialized equipment. Your dog can learn all about it from you, but you need to learn about it from someone else. A basic training course is a must for would-be mushers.

To find out about courses in your area, write to:

> International Federation of Sled Dog Sports
> 1763 Indian Valley Road
> Novato, CA 94947
>
> International Sled Dog Racing Association
> PO Box 446
> Norman, ID 83848-0446

You'll need to start by getting your dog accustomed to the harnesses. Assuming you've completed a basic training course, fit your harness and run through a short lesson.

Bet You Didn't Know

There is an art to putting on a harness. I learned this from Frank Hall, a sled craftsman in Michigan who sold me my first rig. Bunch the harness in your right hand. Offering your dog a treat held between the pinkie and third finger of your right hand, slip the harness over his head just as he accepts the treat, saying "Head Up." Next, lift one paw at a time into the leg fittings, saying "Lift Left" or "Lift Right."

Spread the harness over your dog's back and give him a hug!

Training your dog to the sled is a slow process. You can fit a three-month-old dog to a puppy harness, but don't ask him to pull anything over his own weight until he's eight months old.

Initially you can attach a ten-inch piece of two-by-four to his rig by screwing two eye bolts into the wood and tying the rope to secure it evenly to the harness. The first time you introduce him to pulling weight you should have a partner near the wood to make sure it doesn't get stuck.

To get a dog started on pulling:

➤ Keep your dog on a long lead and stand at his head. Say "Hike" as you lead him forward.

➤ If your dog wants to run say "Easy" and keep him at a walk.

➤ If he turns to look at the wood say "Ep, ep" gently as you continue forward.

➤ Many dogs graduate from a two-by-four to a tire or log. Follow the same procedure, asking a partner to make sure the tire pulls freely. Your careful training procedures will ensure your dog learns to pull correctly.

Once your dog's comfortable in harness, you can introduce some of the commands you'll be using on the trail.

➤ Gee: Right turn

➤ Haw: Left turn

➤ Gee Over: Move to the right or bear right at a fork. In competition this is used to pass another sled on the right.

➤ Haw Over: Move to the left or bear left at a fork. In competition this is used to pass another sled on the left.

> **Sarah Says**
> Train in a clear field or a golf course, so your dog doesn't get snagged or tangled up by all sorts of objects.

When your sled arrives, you'll need to sand it and coat it with a waterproofing material. This project should be shared with your dog; unfortunately, there's no way to teach your dog to handle a paint brush, but you should keep him stationed nearby so that he can bond to your toy, too.

Before hooking the sled up, ask a partner to walk behind it to keep it steady. Hitch your dog to the sled using the proper lines, then put him on a long lead and stand beside him. Repeat the same procedure you practiced with the tire; to begin, run only in straight lines. After a few days you can start using Gee Over. Once your dog starts leading you, practice Haw Over. Then start intermixing the two, but not too often. Only Hike should be repeated frequently. Telling your dog to turn every five seconds is impractical and annoying.

Start your dog out with an empty sled, just to let her get used to the idea.

After a week of beginner practice you can introduce your dog to pace changes, turns, and pulling in front.

For changes of pace, get your dog to move faster by repeating Hike or commanding Hike On. To slow him use Easy, and to stop say Whoa. You already know the commands for right and left. Practice turns in just one direction for a few days, then switch to the other.

By now your dog should be pretty psyched to pull his rig. To get him to pull in front, start your usual Hike at your dog's side, then drop the lead and drift back, repeating Hike. If your dog worries, you may be going too fast. If he's just a worrier, have a human friend stand twenty feet away and clap.

Practice your control commands running four feet behind your dog; if he's confused go on up and help him out. If he makes the transition, praise him wildly, say Whoa, and give him a hug. Yes!

Progressively drift back until you're able to command from behind the sled. If at any point your dog is confused, either slow up a step or have a friend lead your dog while you command him from behind.

When the dog's pulling in front, you get to ride!

Team Stuff and Competition

What's the first thing you think of when someone says dog sled competition? I don't know about you, but I think Iditarod, that grueling 1,150-mile race from Anchorage to Nome, Alaska. The human competitors spend their every waking moment breeding, caring, and training their dogs, who are arctic athletes extraodinaire.

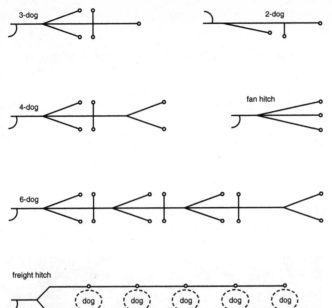

There are plenty of ways to hitch up a dog team.

However, the Iditarod is not all there is. Across the United States a huge variety of sledding events are sponsored each year. These competitions may be short or long, regulated for few dogs or many, lightweight or heavy, recreational or for serious contenders only. To get a listing of sledding events in this country, you can write to the two associations I mentioned previously.

Though I'm assuming you aren't reading this with a team of Siberian Huskies resting on your couch, I want to give you a quick rundown of the terminology and placement of professional teams.

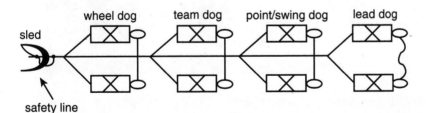

This is how a pro team is hitched up.

➤ **Lead Dogs.** These dogs are the brains of the whole system. Strong and willful, they are tremendously loyal to their driver and are respected by the other dogs. Frank Hall once told me lead dogs are born, not trained.

➤ **Point or Swing Dogs.** Second string lead dogs, these guys are fast and strong.

209

➤ **Team Dogs.** These characters love to pull. They are strength, drive, and desire rolled into one.

➤ **Motor or Wheel Dogs.** Strong and slow, these dogs bear the weight of the sled, keeping it steady and on course.

One last thing: If you want to be a sledder you had better get in shape! Though a team of dogs might be able to pull you along on a leisurely outing, a one-dog sled requires as much pushing as pulling, plus a whole lot of running. Happy trails!

Skijoring

If you're a cross-country ski buff, here's one way to get up those nasty hills: Let your dog pull you up. Yes, it's actually a sport, and it's called skijoring.

Cross country skiing is a lot easier when your dog pulls.

Skijoring probably started in Norway as a way of travel. R. Randel Son wrote that in Norwegian "skijor" means "to plow snow with your face," which is an all too common sight when first rigging up with your dog.

Two harnesses are necessary for this sport: one for your dog (a lightweight pulling harness and traces are best for this activity) and one for yourself. Wearing your harness around your waist will free your hands to balance with your poles.

From personal experience, the most important command to teach and the hardest to learn is Whoa. Imagine a crisp winter day, fresh snow and a dog just champing at the bit to run. Everything is fine until splat—you end up meeting the snow up close and personal. Whoa would definitely be a help here.

Ask a training partner to lead your dog while you command from the rear. You should wear the skis, your helper should not. Other commands are similar to those discussed in sledding: Hike, Gee, Haw, and so on.

When laying out your clothes, remember that you exercise less skijoring than sledding or skiing solo. You also have a tendency to fall more frequently, which means getting wet. Dress warmly and make sure your outer layers are waterproof. For more information about training your dog for skijoring, the Raymond Thompson company (15815 2nd Pl. West, Lynwood, WA 98036) publishes *Skijoring With Dogs*.

> **Sarah Says**
> Do you have a bunch of dogs that love to run, while you prefer to stand still? One to three dogs can pull one person on cross-country skis. Think about it!

Other Fun in the Snow

Being a big fan of this wet white stuff, when I was a kid I made up game after game to stay out "just a few minutes longer." I'm sharing some of them with you to give you an excuse to stay outside just a bit longer as well. Dogs love the snow, so come on—give in!

Snow Soccer

There is this crazy, incredibly hard object called the indestructible ball. You can find it at pet supply stores or in supply catalogs. Dogs love it in any weather, and I find it especially fun in the snow. You can make up rules or just hack around; your dog won't care one bit.

Tunneling

Dogs love to dig anyway, and at least when they dig in the snow they'll come out clean. If you live where the snow piles high, take your dog out and start digging a tunnel. He's going to think he died and went to heaven. Digging with his best buddy! You can create a tunnel with two openings and teach your dog Hit the Dirt as you dive into the tunnel together!

> **Grrr**
>
> Just because dogs love the snow, it doesn't mean their bodies can regulate cold temperatures. Northern dogs have developed a double-layered coat that insulates them from the cold. But if your dog is a fair weather breed, invest in a sweater and don't leave him alone in the cold. Dogs are nearly as susceptible to frostbite and hypothermia as we are.

King of the Hill

Even if you don't get fifteen inches of snow, the plows always seem to pile it above your head on either side of the street. Those piles make for great adventures and wonderful Kodak moments. All you'll need to do is lead your dog to the snow hill and say Up; up he'll go. Try tossing a snowball up there, and see if your pal can bring it back before it melts in his mouth.

It would be a different world if dogs hibernated, but a lot less interesting. And a lot less fun!

The Least You Need to Know

➤ Dogs of every breed love the snow, but depending on your dog's coat type you may need to watch out for snow packing around the paws and hypothermia. Invest in a good doggie sweater and never leave your dog out alone.

➤ With all these precautions for the dogs, don't forget yourself! Dress warmly, stretch out, and pack a few snacks for quick energy.

➤ Your dog's sled harness must fit correctly, or the dog will certainly be uncomfortable and may be injured.

➤ Start your dog sledding hobby with a quick course in how to use the equipment. You'll be glad you did.

Hit the Road

In This Chapter

➤ Hiking and backpacking with your dog

➤ Hazards to watch out for

➤ Rules of the road

➤ Canine carting

Some of the best times I've had with my dogs have been wandering around on roads and trails. Curious, full of wonder and excitement, dogs are sometimes the best companions. They're not self-sufficient however, so there are some things to keep in mind. In this chapter we'll look at hiking, backpacking canine style, and some things to watch out for on the trail. And for those of you who would rather sit than walk, or who have kids dreaming of their very own dog-drawn carriage, we'll also look into dog carting.

Go Take a Hike

I love hiking. Just ask the dogs. To me there is no more relaxing activity in the world. Hiking, however, is a strenuous activity and not without risks, so if you're going to take a hike, there are a few guidelines I'd encourage you to follow.

The first thing you'll need to do is determine if your dog is healthy enough to hit the trail. If you're not sure, go to your vet. Ask the vet to check your dog's heart, blood, and respiration. If all is well and your dog is game, take him on a short hike near your home. Does he run out of gas? You'll need to do some conditioning. Jogging, tennis ball fetch, and swimming are great ways to get your dog in shape. You, too!

Sarah Says
Watch those pads! If your dog is out of condition, her pads will wear quickly and might even bleed. Aside from conditioning her heart, you'll need to toughen up those toes.

Sarah Says
If you've got a puppy, introduce her to short trail hikes after she's had all her inoculations. Keep her on a ten-foot leash and call her back to you for a treat every few minutes. Also, introduce the command Wait to mean stop in your tracks.

Before you go out on the trail you should make sure your dog's ID tags, rabies inoculation, and license are up-to-date. Tattooing your dog is another option, though please don't tattoo the ear. (People who are sick enough to steal a dog wouldn't think twice about removing the ear so they can sell your dog to a laboratory.)

Respect all trail restrictions. If an area is blocked off, don't go there. If the trail requires all dogs be on leash, comply. Even if it doesn't, leash your dog if she won't stay with you. And *always* pick up after your dog. I know, I know, bears do it in the woods. But dogs should not, especially not on a trail other people will be using.

You may get to an area and find a No Dogs Allowed sign. Quite a disappointment, but it's there for a reason. Sometimes the reason is that other dog owners didn't follow the rules and ruined it for everybody. We don't make the rules, but we should follow them.

Most dog friendly parks will allow dogs that are under voice control to hike off leash. Polish up the Heel, Come, and Down commands, and never let your dog off leash if you have the slightest doubt that she will obey.

Pack It In

I consider backpacking excursions to be more than a day hike. Although the planning is a little more complicated when including your dog, you won't find a better companion. With a little practice you can even teach your dog to carry a pack.

Call the place you are planning to visit and make sure they are dog friendly. Ask politely what their restrictions are and what hazards you should watch for. Please check the following table for common dangers on the trail and how to avoid them.

Common Dangers on the Trail

	Hazard	Safety Precaution
Mice, rats	Rabies, distemper, leptospirosis, salmonella	Keep your dog's vaccinations up-to-date and keep him away from these animals
Rabbits	Dogs chasing rabbits can get lost; even well-trained dogs get distracted and may not heed your commands	Keeping your dog on leash is best; a very loud yell NO may stop your dog from running
Skunks	Skunk spray can act like mace if it gets in your dog's eyes	Flush the eyes with cool water; the smell can be reduced with tomato juice or a commercial product
Opossums	Can spread fleas, ticks, and mites and may attack if threatened	Keep your dog away from them
Raccoons	Will fight with a dog; their bite can spread rabies, distemper, or parvo	Keep your dog's vaccinations up to date and keep him away from these animals
Porcupines	Their quills can lodge in a dog and continue to work into the body until they pierce an organ	Keep your dog away from them; quills must be removed by a veterinarian
Bears	If left alone, bears usually pose no threat; but if startled or annoyed, an attack can be deadly	Hike with bear bells to warn them off and keep your dog on leash; if you see a bear, make a lot of noise
Alligators	They are very fast and can surprise a dog; an attack can be fatal	Keep your dog away from water in areas where alligators are present
Snakes	The bite of a poisonous snake can be fatal	Stay away from snakes; if your dog is bitten, get to a vet immediately
Lizards, toads, spiders	Some varieties are coated with poison that can kill if they are bitten	Keep your dog away from them; to treat, induce vomiting and get to a vet immediately
People	Hunting accidents, trash, poison, leg traps	Your dog should be at your side and on a leash

continues

continued

	Hazard	Safety Precaution
Heat	Heat exhaustion; dehydration; heat stroke with vomiting and weakness	Bring plenty of water and give your dog a drink often; treat by wrapping dog in wet clothing and dripping water into his mouth; bring to vet immediately
Sun	Sunburn, especially skin on ears and nose	Use nontoxic sunblock and a damp towel draped over the back and sides of a shorthaired dog
Ice	Can cut paws	Trim hair around toes to prevent ice balls from forming
Cold	Hypothermia, accompanied by lethargy, uncontrolled shivering, or unconsciousness	Invest in a good dog sweater and watch your dog carefully; treat by lying next to your dog in a sleeping bag
Lakes, streams	Drowning in undercurrents; snags on underwater branches; parasites from drinking	Never let a dog swim in a strong current, and remove all collars except for close-fitting ID; bring your own supply of drinking water
Plants	Watch for thorns, thistles, burrs, poison ivy, cactus	Keep your dog out of obvious patches and check his whole body carefully after every hike
Fleas, ticks	Ehrlichiosis, Lyme disease, Rocky Mountain spotted fever, plague, infection, and more	Use flea and tick repellents, and check his whole body carefully after every hike

To teach your dog to carry a pack you must first get one that fits properly. I've noticed some high-quality packs in many outdoor gear catalogs and dog magazines. Before investing in one, ask the dealer what material will be resting against your dog's back and where the clasps lie. A breathable material such as nylon mesh is best, and the clasps should rest behind your dog's elbow, not on her stomach.

When teaching your dog to carry a pack, let her get used to wearing it without weight for a few days. Next, stuff it full of tissue paper and lead your dog on a walk around the house on a leash. Next, balance your dog's packs with two light objects of equal weight and go for a walk outside. Correct any attempts to rub or scratch the pack, saying "Ep, ep" and moving forward happily.

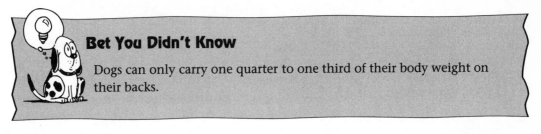

Bet You Didn't Know

Dogs can only carry one quarter to one third of their body weight on their backs.

Progressively lengthen your walks and increase the weight to your dog's weight capacity. Eventually your dog will be happy to see the pack because it means you're going for a long walk. When you get to this stage, you're ready to hit the trail.

Making Camp

Though most people who backpack also camp, not all people who camp also backpack. Got it? I mean, some people just drive to the campgrounds. I point this out because there's a reason I made this a separate section.

The first word I think of when someone says "camping" is fire. That's probably because my favorite part of a camping trip is the food. Your dog, however, must be protected from campfires. I recommend creating a safety zone for your dog that's well out of range of stray sparks that could land on his coat. Fifteen feet is a good distance. Station your dog there on a leash with a familiar bed and toy. You're welcome to eat next to your dog, just don't cook next to him.

While most campgrounds are dog friendly, some aren't. Others limit the number of pets per campsite. Your best bet is to check out the rules a few weeks ahead of time. If the site will not accept your dog, you'll have time to find another place to camp, rather than leaving home without your dog.

Here are a few other pretrip preparations:

- ❏ Update all ID, license, and inoculation tags, and pack all paperwork.
- ❏ Check your dog's collar, leash, pack, and any other equipment.
- ❏ Pack familiar beds, crates, toys, and bowls.
- ❏ Take plenty of food and water and don't forget any medications. Changing any of these things may stress your dog's system.
- ❏ Prepare for all emergencies: Pack first aid materials, flea and tick sprays, and skunk off.

❏ If you're traveling in cold weather, pack a sweater, extra towels, and blankets to warm your dog, if necessary.

❏ Last but not least, tuck in a pile of poop bags.

Die-hard campers spend many moons under the stars and many days out on the trails. If you bring your dog, remember you're part of a large and loving population of dog owners. To place us in the best light, make sure you control your dog. Keep him on a leash when necessary, clean up after him, control the barking, and be courteous to your neighbors. Your good manners reflect on us all.

Canine Carting

For those of us who always dreamed of owning a pony and cart, canine carting is a nice alternative. The only prerequisite is a dog that loves to pull. Size doesn't matter. Breed has nothing to do with it. Competition is purely an option. Your dog can pull a cart to take the trash out, clean the yard, bring in firewood, or take the kids for a ride.

Before you start, your dog must be trained in the basics: Heel, Sit, Stand, Down, Stay, and so on. Other good words to teach your dog before your harness arrives are Left, Right, Fast, Slow, and Back.

Before I give you an overview of the training process, let's discuss equipment.

The Harness

You'll need a harness for your dog. If you thought she was powerful at the end of a leash, just wait until you get her in one of these things.

Front Girth. This piece stabilizes the harness and helps distribute the weight evenly across the chest and shoulders.

V1. This piece must fit snugly on your dog's chest. It distributes the weight over the shoulders. The V should rest at your dog's breast bone.

V2. The second V meets at your dog's withers. It must never fall behind the shoulders, as that would put too much strain on the back.

Shaft Loop. Positioned at the shoulder, this piece balances the cart and prevents it from rolling forward into your dog.

Side Straps. These serve to balance the harness on the dog and help distribute the weight evenly.

Traces. These connect to the cart.

Rear Girth. This piece centers the harness and falls on your dog's thighs.

Wagon harnesses, which would allow your dog to pull more weight (good for the kids!) differ from the carting harness in that they have a chest strap that distributes the weight forward and a girth strap that positions the harness on your dog. In place of the rear girth there is a prepared bar that should be placed under your dog's tail to rest on her thighs. This piece attaches to the *single tree* of the wagon.

Carts and Wagons

The difference between a cart and a wagon is that carts have two wheels and turn nicely, but don't balance heavy loads well. Wagons have four wheels and distribute weight evenly so the dog won't feel off balance, but they are a bit awkward to turn. Wagons do well at county fairs and for heavy yard work. Carts are good for training and competition, coming in lightweight versions up to fifty-pound competition style. Wagons, though heavier, can be constructed out of your garden variety wagon or bought from a reputable source. Check carting magazines and newsletters for the best places to buy.

Bet You Didn't Know

For more information about carting, try *Cart and Sled Dog Training* by Raymond Thompson, 15815 2nd Pl. West, Lynwood, WA 98036; or the carting information packet put out by the Newfoundland Club of America (your dog need not be a Newf), NCA Land Work Secretary Roger Powell, 5208 Olive Rd., Raleigh, NC 27606.

The shafts are the pieces that attach to the shaft loops on your dog's harness. An adjustable break on the shaft keeps the wagon from rolling into your dog. The single tree, which transforms a wagon into a dog wagon, hooks up to the traces and keeps the harness in balance.

Putting the Dog Before the Cart

The first step in training is familiarizing your dog with the harness. Once she accepts having it put on, she should wear it while you review her basic training: stress Stand, Sit, Down and Stay, Left and Right, Fast and Slow, and Back.

Grrr
Before transforming that old wagon gathering dust in the garage, turn it around in a circle. Does one wheel stay under the bed while the other projects out? No good. This forces the weight of the load onto three wheels, tossing everything (including your dog) off balance. When wagons turn, all four wheels must stay under the flat bed.

Teaching your dog to back up may sound easier than it is. Backward is not a direction your dog is used to moving in. To teach her, set up a two-by-four-foot chute in your home (some chairs along a wall will do). Make sure to bring some of your dog's favorite treats. Standing in the opening facing your dog, hold the treat along her jaw line and shuffle your feet toward her as you say "Back." If she steps back with even one foot, congratulate her. If she sits, no dice. If you are having trouble, check where you are holding her treat; it must be along her jaw line. If all else fails, have a training partner *gently* hold her back end up as you encourage her backward.

Get your dog used to pulling something light, such as a log, before you introduce the cart.

When your dog has all of the basics down, you can begin training.

➤ Place empty traces on her and walk along in a straight line.

➤ Next, attach a light weight to the traces. Try a large paper bag stuffed with newspaper. Have a training partner walk by the bag as you steady your dog forward. If she's concerned, encourage her along and keep walking.

Sarah Says

If your dog is disturbed by the cart, go back a few steps and work at it slowly. During practice, reinforce the steps that your dog is comfortable with before working on the tough stuff. When you come to the tough stuff, use plenty of treats.

➤ Attach a heavier item on the traces, such as a two-by-four plank. To ensure the weight is distributed evenly, secure two eye bolts and ropes to the wood plank. At this stage you should be focusing your dog with treats and your partner should be watching the plank to ensure it doesn't get caught.

➤ When first introducing the cart to your dog, you should explore it together. Wait until your dog is comfortable with her new toy before hitching her up.

➤ Your partner will be an integral part of the training for a while, so don't plan a session without him or her. The first step in teaching your dog to walk with the cart is to have your partner hold the shafts of the cart and walk it in place next to your dog. Steady your dog using the term Forward. Teaching your dog to turn with the cart comes later, so you and your dog should turn separately for now.

Let your dog sniff and explore the empty cart with you before you hitch her up.

➤ Next, your partner should occasionally bump into your dog with the shafts while walking next to her. Watch your dog's reaction, keeping her moving along as if it was no big deal. Continue to turn separately.

➤ Your partner must be around the day you place your dog into the shafts. At first place the shafts into the loops only and walk along while your partner steadies the shafts. You can now introduce the words Pull and Halt. Do not turn with the cart yet.

➤ Now you're ready to connect the traces to the single tree. Your helper should still hold the shafts to keep them steady.

➤ Without your partner, rig your dog and practice your stationary obedience commands: Stand, Sit, Down, and Stay.

➤ Still working in a straight line, command Pull, Halt, Wait, Fast, and Slow. In that order! Make sure your dog has mastered one concept before introducing the next.

Sarah Says
If you've got a big dog, you may need a weighted cart to introduce commands such as Fast, Slow, and Halt. Remember, with carts the weight must be evenly distributed. You can purchase weight bars made especially for this purpose.

➤ To teach your dog turns you should work in an open parking lot or cul de sac. Start with big left circles, saying Left as you herd your dog to the side and lure her with food. Do this until you're sure your dog is having fun with it. Slowly work in smaller circles. Now do the same thing to the right.

Sarah Says

If you're planning kid rides or yard help, wagons are a must. A cart would not be able to balance the weight and if it tips, you might scare your dog off carting for good.

➤ The last thing your dog should learn before you take the show on the road is backing up. Of course, she must know what you're talking about before you ask for it in harness. Calling your partner back to straighten the cart while your dog backs up is useful. It can also help to practice on an uphill slope, where gravity encourages your dog to back up. Soon it will be part of the show.

Once your dog is accustomed to the cart, you can acclimate her more quickly to a wagon, or just have fun with your cart.

The Least You Need to Know

➤ Make sure your dog is healthy enough to go hiking. Have him checked by a vet, and make sure he has all his inoculations, ID tags, and up-to-date licenses.

➤ Check in advance to make sure your destination is dog friendly.

➤ Buy high-quality equipment that is safe for your dog and fits properly. This goes for hiking, carting, and everything else.

➤ Take along an ample supply of the food and water your dog already knows and loves.

➤ Always be a responsible dog owner. Keep your dog under control and clean up after him.

➤ Any healthy dog can get into carting. Just make sure you put the right size cart behind the dog.

Part 5
Encore!

Now that you've expanded your repertoire and stuffed your sleeves with new tricks and special routines, I'll need to get you out in the public eye. Whether you volunteer at a school, visit a nursing home, share a booth with an animal shelter at a local fair, or you want to put on your sunglasses and head for Hollywood, the chapters in this last section will give you some direction. Don't be frustrated if you're not discovered overnight...if I've learned one thing in the dog training business, it's that everything takes time.

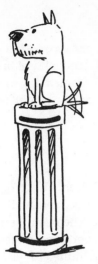

Chapter 23

Pillar of the Community

In This Chapter

➤ How to get your dog used to performing in public

➤ Certification programs for Good Citizens and canine therapists

➤ Teaching the next generation

➤ How to get involved in community events

Now that you've polished your routine, you might want to think about sharing your pride and joy with those around you. From nursing homes to community events, your pet will be recognized and adored wherever you go. People won't even bother with you anymore; they'll direct their entire conversation to your dog (who they'll know by name).

What's in it for you? The satisfaction of getting involved in something enjoyable, making a difference in someone's life, showing off your dog training skills....

Get Out of the House

Before volunteering your time, get recognized. Take your dog out on a Saturday and practice your tricks on the street corner or in the park. No soliciting please! Just have some fun and see who you attract. People love to watch a well-trained dog in action. It may take a few weeks, but try to establish a following in your neighborhood before you start offering your services.

Canine Good Citizen™ Test

Next you'll want to get your dog certified as a Canine Good Citizen. This program, called CGC for short, is a noncompetitive test developed to recognize and certify dogs and their owners as responsible citizens of their community. Although this test was developed and is promoted by the American Kennel Club, it is not limited to pure-bred dogs. Mixed breeds are encouraged to certify as well.

Sarah Says
Working your dog in public also ensures that he'll work in front of a crowd. Don't be discouraged if it takes him a while to perform at the same level he's capable of at home. Patience is a dog trainer's top virtue.

This test measures a dog's social skills and public manners, and is not a competition. The goal of the CGC test is not to eliminate participants, but to encourage pet owners to learn the skills necessary to train their dogs to be safe, mannerly members of our society.

In order to pass the test, your dog must know the commands Heel, Sit, Down, and Stay. The test is comprised of ten evaluations:

1. **Accepting a Friendly Stranger.** To pass this test the dog must allow a nonthreatening person to approach and speak to the handler.

2. **Sitting Politely for Petting.** The dog must allow a friendly stranger to pet him while sitting at his handler's side.

3. **Appearance and Grooming.** The dog must be clean and well-groomed, and must allow a stranger (representing a veterinarian or groomer) to handle and groom him without suspicion.

4. **Out for a Walk.** The dog must walk attentively at the handler's side. To pass this evaluation the dog does not have to heel perfectly or sit when the handler is instructed to stop.

5. **Walking Through a Crowd.** The dog must be attentive to his owner and in control as he is lead through a crowd of people.

6. **Sit and Down on Command/Staying in Place.** The dog must respond to the handler's Sit, Down, and Stay commands.

7. **Praise/Interaction.** The dog must calm down within ten seconds after praise and interaction.

8. **Reaction to Another Dog.** The dog must be in control and focused on the handler while passing another dog.

9. **Reaction to Distractions.** The dog must remain calm and confident when faced with everyday distractions. The distractions at an evaluation might include a child running, a bicyclist, or a person on crutches or in a wheelchair.

10. **Supervised Isolation.** For this test the dog is fastened to a six-foot line and is expected to wait calmly when his handler disappears for three minutes.

I am a certified CGC evaluator and give this test to my college (dog college) graduates. It is a fun way for everyone to measure their success.

Bet You Didn't Know

If you think you and your dog are ready for the CGC test, contact the American Kennel Club at the address below to find a program in your area.

Canine Good Citizen Program
5580 Centerview Drive, Suite 200
Raleigh, NC 27606
(919) 233-9780

Pet Therapy

No dogs on the couch please; this is not about doggie psychiatrists. Pet therapy is the involvement of well-trained dogs in therapeutic situations such as in nursing homes, children's centers, prisons, and other long-term care facilities. I've been doing it for years and it never stops amazing me how the unconditional love of a dog can light up a person's life and ease his or her interactions with the world around them.

Before you call up and offer your services, you need to learn about how pet therapy works. I remember my first pet therapy class, which I took in New York City with my beloved dog Kyia. Together we were exposed to many of the unfamiliar situations that we would eventually encounter on our therapy visits.

When someone is feeling lonely and depressed, sometimes only a dog can get through to them.

Now I have a class I run to socialize dogs to the rigors of these environments. The dogs are exposed to wheelchairs, walkers, metal objects, a variety of handling techniques, speech patterns, and people of all ages. Before these dogs are allowed to go visiting, I certify them with Therapy Dogs International (TDI). This organization provides ID cards with both the person's and the dog's picture on it. Originally developed to raise the level of training and professionalism required to ensure a dog's readiness for this type of work, TDI now provides insurance for its members. As of 1995 I became a certified evaluator of Therapy Dogs, which is to say that I decide what dogs are ready to apply for certification. It's both a responsibility and an honor.

Grrr

Not everyone is a dog lover. If you're out visiting and someone says they don't want to meet your dog, don't push it. Often this is one of the few choices left to people in care facilities. Respect that.

If you have a dog who is social and loving, yet calm and well-mannered, you may find this activity very rewarding. Although many facilities welcome volunteers, it is best to take a class or work with someone who is familiar with the rigors of the therapeutic situations before committing yourself. Even the most even-tempered dogs can become startled or stressed when they are faced with an unfamiliar experience. By exposing your dog to every possible situation that might occur, he'll better be able to cope with the unexpected.

Bet You Didn't Know

You can contact Therapy Dogs International at:

6 Hilltop Road
Mendham, NJ 07945

A good book to read about getting started in pet therapy is *Volunteering With Your Pet* by Dr. Mary Burch (Howell Book House, New York).

Back to School

I remember a school assembly when I was in third grade. Three Golden Retrievers came out individually and worked through retrieving exercises, then worked together—hand signals only. Their trainer also talked to us about dog safety: How to approach strange dogs, how to act if approached by an unleashed dog, and the importance of taking care of the dog you own. Needless to say, it made a huge impression on me.

If extending yourself to the next generation sounds good to you, call up a local school. Ask for the name of the person in charge of assemblies and activities. Give them a quick briefing and ask if you can send them a proposal for a school program you'd like to give.

Now it's time to whip out the old pencil and pad, or computer, and put on your thinking cap. A good proposal includes:

Grrr
Maybe I'm being a little over-cautious here, but make sure your dog is super child friendly before you even consider contacting a school.

➤ Your name, address, and phone number.

➤ Your dog's name.

➤ A photo of you and your dog(s), if you have one: Here I am with my pal Beauty.

➤ A short paragraph giving background information on the dog's training and certifications and any prior work with children.

➤ Who you'd like to speak to. Do you want to pack an auditorium? Would you rather go class to class? Do you want to work with a special population within the school, such as learning disabled children or the science class? Think it through.

➤ What information you'd like to present. Dog safety and responsible care should be high on your list.

➤ What you hope to accomplish by coming to the school.

Print the description on nice paper and outline it neatly. For example, you could have headings for each of the sections:

➤ About Me

➤ About My Dog

➤ Our Background

➤ Program Proposal

➤ Message

Enclose a short note thanking the school for taking the time to consider your proposal and saying that you will follow up this letter with a phone call in one week. They will be impressed with your professionalism.

Kids' Parties

This dog for hire. If you've got an act that's really hot and both you and your dog get a kick hanging out with children, this is a great way to get a happy return on all your hard work. Think about it: Which would you rather have at your kid's birthday party—a purple dinosaur or a trained dog?

There are two people in my area who offer this unique entertainment. One brings an entire petting zoo, including her star trick dog Twinkle. The other comes with her three dogs, and after a stellar performance she lets them socialize with the kids.

If you're a novice trainer, you might want to apprentice with a more experienced party animal for a while. Kids are a chaotic crew, and they can shake even the steadiest of dogs. So be sure your pal is old reliable before you start advertising your services.

Fairs and Local Events

Okay, so you and your trickster have the charm to attract a crowd. So now what? Renting a booth at a community event with an animal shelter or to promote a charity can be a great outlet to put your trick work to some good use.

For a community rundown of events, contact your local Chamber of Commerce or Town Hall. Parades and fairs usually occur in the warmer weather and are often held in honor of some holiday, such as Thanksgiving, Memorial Day, or Labor Day. Schools also hold benefit functions and would love to have animal acts as part of their fun. Check it out.

Once you've got the schedule, you'll need to do some planning. Booths are a big deal and usually cost money. But many groups that are exhibiting anyway would love to have you volunteer your time to be there. If your dog is a real ham, they may even publicize his act at a certain time to attract attention to your performance.

Local events are a good place to show off what you and your pal know. That's me and Kyia on stage.

Here's a list of animal groups to consider approaching to share booth space:

➤ Local animal shelters

➤ Renowned dog groups, for example, Guiding Eyes for the Blind or Companions for Independence

➤ Pet supply stores

➤ Animal hospitals

➤ Local dog enthusiasts or business operators (groomers or trainers)

➤ Dog clubs

Sarah Says
Every time you show off your well-trained trickster, you're playing your part in making the world a more dog-friendly place.

Years ago the Mount Kisco Chamber of Commerce (near where I live) held its annual Sales Days in July and publicized my participation. It drew dog lovers from surrounding towns and I had a great time showing off my beautiful Husky Kyia.

The Least You Need to Know

➤ Go out and get recognized. Practice your tricks and activities in public.

➤ If you have a friendly, social dog, consider training her for pet therapy. Nothing brightens a day more than the unconditional love of a dog.

➤ If your dog loves kids, call up your local school and offer to come and put on a show or talk to the students about dog safety.

➤ If you're considering participating in any public activity, make sure your dog is well-trained, well-socialized, and reliable. A certification program is the best way to test your trickster before you get to work.

Lights, Camera, Action!

So you think your dog is one hot number? Hoping you'll be able to retire and send your four-footed pal out to bring home the bacon? Don't quit your job just yet. You've got more competition out there than you can imagine, and breaking down those Hollywood doors requires more than just a pretty face.

Don't get me wrong; if you think you've got what it takes, if your dog is a real ham with her tricks, give it a shot. In this chapter we'll go over what you need to know to get started in show biz, and what to say so you'll sound like a true professional.

Preparing Your Pro

First order of business—your dog. Sure, she may be a living-room wonder, but that doesn't mean she'll perform under blazing studio lights. Then there's you to worry about. Can you sweat it out when strange eyes are upon you? Can you stay cool when the Great Oz of the camera crew is making demands? If you buckle, so will your dog.

Bet You Didn't Know

The hardest thing to control on stage is not your dog, it's you. We humans are a nervous bunch when it comes to performance under pressure, and your dog will reflect whatever tension you exude. But remember, your dog will also reflect your calm attitude. So keep it cool!

Before you send out a dozen portfolios or waste any money on long distance phone calls to Los Angeles, New York, or Chicago, let's see if you and your dog have got what it takes.

➤ Bring some big lights into your living room. If you don't have any camera lights handy, go down to your local hardware store and buy an outdoor spot light. Does your dog cower when there is a glare in her eyes? Can you work beyond this?

➤ Bring some neighbors in to watch you and your dog perform. Try working at a distance and using hand signals only.

➤ Work your dog around distractions. Have some family members or friends really whoop it up in the next room, opening outside doors, and laughing in spite of themselves.

➤ Find a stage or walkway and work your dog around the edge. It would be a real bummer to get your big break and have your best pal quit because she couldn't deal with her sense of depth perception.

Sarah Says
If your dog is disturbed by the big, bright lights of film or stage, don't despair! You could still have a future in advertising; whether local or worldwide, seeing your dog in print is a real thrill.

Does your dog's concentration waver? If so, you'll need to work through any problems she has before you take the next step.

Next, you'll need to take your show on the road. Go practice on a street corner, strengthening your Stay command and your ability to control your dog from a distance. Accentuate your hand signals and encourage your dog's focus no matter what's going on around you. Read Chapter 23 and volunteer to perform your act at a school or nursing home, just to get used to working in front of strangers.

Getting Recognized

Now that your act is rock solid, you need recognition.

Making yourself known in the industry is not an easy or quick process. First, you should get professional photographs of your dog to send around with your portfolio. Black and whites are traditional and are still respected in film, stage, and advertising. Then you need to get work of any kind just for the experience. Let's discuss some options.

Professional photos of you and your dog really make an impression. Here I am with Beauty the Bulldog.

Advertising

Start by studying both local and national newspapers, catalogs, and magazines. Cut out the ads that use dogs and get a feel for the positions and messages the dog in the ad is trying to convey. Clothing catalogs use dogs to convey a sporty, country attitude. Ads with children often have a "mayhem" suburban feel. Destination shots usually show the dog as part of the home you've left behind. Some ads use dogs in unusual situations, just to catch your eye.

Now cut out ads you feel could be made better if they had a dog. List three reasons why a dog could improve the picture and draw more attention to the product. For example, I'm looking at an ad that is trying to sell jogging shoes. There is this gorgeous guy in the ad, wearing a T-shirt and moist with perspiration. He is leaning over tying his brand new sneaker. Here are three ways a dog could improve this ad:

> **Sarah Says**
> Doggy bags are essential when you're planning a full working day. Pack a water bottle and a dish, a spray bottle with water to cool your dog off in hot weather, a meal if you're going to be out all day (for you and your dog), a familiar mat to lie on, and a favorite chew toy.

1. Dogs capture attention and bring out a softer side of a man.

2. Dogs give a sporty feel.

3. People who run are outdoorsy types, and most outdoorsy types like dogs.

Laurie is cute, but she's even cuter with her dog.

Also, consider the color of your dog's coat and find ads that would highlight her natural beauty. Are you getting a feel for this? Okay then, you are ready for your next steps. As with all great things, you start small and build.

➤ Look in your local paper and find an advertisement you feel could be improved by placing your dog in the picture.

➤ Write down your list of exactly how and why.

➤ Contact the merchant, either by writing him a letter and enclosing your photos or, if you live in a small town, simply going into the store. (If you write, make sure you say that you'll be contacting him at the beginning of the following week. *Then do it.*)

Sarah Says
Let your local merchants know that you'd be willing to do the first ad for free. *Yes, I said free!* Any famous person will have racks of performances he or she did just to get experience.

➤ If you go in, buy something from the store and ask to speak with the owner. Let him know how much you thought of his ad, how it gave you great ideas ("See, I even bought something!"). Then tell him about your idea to use your dog in his ad, and how it will attract a broader audience.

➤ If he seems interested, offer to show your photos and bring your dog around.

If one merchant doesn't bite, try another and keep trying until you land your first job. Once you get your first ad, start to make a professional portfolio.

Take the Stage

Of course, to be on Broadway you have to live in or near New York. But a stage is a stage is a stage, and if you think you and your dog might enjoy live performances, I'm sure you can find one. Although you can't put a dog into a play that doesn't call for one, you can locate the theaters surrounding your home and find out what plays will be performed during the year. If they call for a dog, apply early by sending your portfolio, resume, and photos.

Just to warn you, theater is the most demanding occupation for a dog and it doesn't pay enough to feed a Poodle. It also requires incredible patience and composure on your part. Make sure you and your dog are both up to it!

Sarah Says
If you're into stage work, make sure your dog is used to working on platforms and won't get nervous near the edge.

The Silver Screen

Commercials, television, movies—the big time! Getting your dog on the set of a film or TV spot is a long shot. But that's what dreams are made of, so let me wish you luck!

Getting your first break is no small order. Your best bet will be to sign on with an animal agency in a local city. If the nearest city is 300 miles away however, that may be a challenge.

For those of you who want to try it on your own, you'll need to locate and send your material to a local film office, which handles all screen work coming into your state. Keeping the film commissioner updated on the status of your dog keeps your name on the list of people to contact when the big show comes to town.

Bet You Didn't Know

The first dog to appear on the silver screen was a German Shepherd named Strongheart who starred in a 1921 film *The Silent Call*. Unfortunately for him, his fame was usurped the following year when Rin Tin Tin appeared on the scene, fresh from the trenches of the first World War.

Finding an Agent

If you want to be a free agent with your dog, don't forget that you'll be out there swimming with the sharks. Finding an agent to represent you can be a wise idea, especially if you are trying to break into the film industry. Once you sign with an agent, they will be in charge of negotiating all deals and all you'll have to do is sit by the phone and wait. Here are some things to keep in mind when you are looking for an agent:

➤ Look for an agent who is experienced in dealing with people on all levels of the entertainment industry, from the script writers to the actors to the director.

➤ If the agency will be handling your dog directly, make sure it has been licensed by the United States Department of Agriculture.

➤ Find an agent you feel comfortable with and who will explain the negotiating process, should you ever find yourself cornered.

Finding an agent is no picnic. I know, I know…you have the world's most charming ball of fur lapping water from your toilet, but remember you've got competition out there!

Sarah Says
If your dog is a real trickster, try to get a high-quality video tape made to show to agents and producers. They like to know what the dog is capable of doing.

Think of it as your first adventure. Network, network. Ask all your friends in the dog world; ask them who they know or who they might know. If you come up empty handed, you'll need to go in cold. Write up a nice cover letter introducing yourself, your dog and your accomplishments. Send photos, a portfolio if you have one, and a professionally produced two-minute video of your furry star. At the end of your cover letter, let the agent know you will be calling her office to follow up. And when you call, get a feel for her personality and time constraints before you push for a personal meeting.

Show Me the Money

Negotiating money can be a tricky thing. If you have an agent, you can expect her to negotiate financial contracts for you. If not, remember the golden rule of negotiation: You can always lower your asking price, but you can never raise it.

That said, don't expect to make a lot of money when you're starting out. Local advertising and stage work probably won't pay a thing, but in the beginning the experience will be worth more than the money. For stock photos you may get a small advance, and you'll receive royalties if your dog is chosen.

> ### Bet You Didn't Know
>
> For a list of film offices in your area, advice on negotiating film and commercial fees, and just about anything else you'll need to know, pick up Capt. Arthur J. Haggerty's book *How to Get Your Pet Into Show Business* (Howell Book House, New York). This excellent reference will expand on all the ins and outs of the show biz world, as well as provide you with an invaluable address book.

The Truth

The truth is, whether your dog makes the final cut or you're left standing outside in the pouring rain, you still have one thing no one else in the world has: your dog. And whether or not anyone else recognizes it, your dog is your star.

Please, no matter how many rejections you endure, no matter how many times he ignores your direction when the moment counts, don't ever let your dog forget how much he means to you. Dogs were not born to be exploited, and exploitation is the stepchild of the advertising and film industry. Your dog was not born to be just another pretty face in a commercial, he was born to be loved.

Your dog is always your star.

The Least You Need to Know

➤ If you think your dog truly has what it takes to be a star, you first need to put it to the test by seeing if your dog can perform under hot lights and in front of strangers.

➤ Local advertisements can be a good way to build your portfolio.

➤ Always be calm and professional, and your dog will be, too.

➤ Think of your attempts to get noticed as an adventure. If it works, cool. If it doesn't, well, you've still got your dog and that's more than anyone else can say!

Happy Tails to You

In This Chapter

➤ Your dog's true worth

➤ What we all learn from dogs

Sure your dog may never star in a commercial or he may be too embarrassed to show off his routines at the local Elks Club, but that doesn't rob you of the one undeniable fact: If you love your dog, he's a star. And the size of your star is not measured by how many people share your pride, it's measured by you.

When I listen to some of my friends and clients talk about their dogs, whether it be a tale of mischief or one of training, I feel the warmth in their hearts, and when I see the dog face-to-face I already know that dog's worth.

Canine Ambassador

I always say, a well-trained dog is an ambassador for us all. Whether you're just clowning around in your living room or you're putting on an act at a local fair, the work and time you've devoted to your dog will shine through wherever you take him.

You'll be surprised at the doors you will be able to open with the simplest of tricks. Children, otherwise terrified of dogs, will delight in a well-mannered trickster. People with no time for the four-footed will look on in wonder. And those of us who love our dogs as much as you do will congratulate you on your efforts toward making the world a more dog-friendly place.

Strictly Optional, Strictly Fun

Many people have asked me why I decide to write this book. An editor and old friend of mine even went so far as to warn me off the project, saying that a book about tricks would hurt my reputation as a serious trainer. Too late now!

Reputation or not, I gave my editor the same answer I give everyone else: I wrote this book for the fun of it. It was fun for me; I needed a break from the heel and housebreaking. And hopefully, it has been fun for you. After all, having fun with your dog usually tops the list of reasons we share our lives with dogs in the first place.

They bring us back to a time when pleasure was our only priority; when having a good time and being loved unconditionally was the name of the game.

I guess the most special thing about writing this book, what makes it different from the other training books I've written, is that this one is optional. Nobody has to teach their dog tricks. No one needs to get involved in activity training. After all, it's time consuming, sometimes costly, and requires incredible patience and understanding. But if you have chosen to go this extra mile, I know that your relationship with your dog is a special one, unique from all the others. Your dog is your gift, and in turn you have chosen to give back to him.

Happy tails to you. 'Til we meet again!

That's me with some of my star pupils.

More to Read

General Care and Training

Burnham, Patricia Gail, *Playtraining Your Dog,* New York: St. Martins Press, 1980.

Carlson, Delbert, DVM and James Giffin, MD, *Dog Owner's Home Veterinary Handbook,* New York: Howell Book House, 1992.

DeBitetto, James, DVM and Sarah Hodgson, *You and Your Puppy*, New York: Howell Book House, 1995.

Hodgson, Sarah, *The Complete Idiot's Guide to Choosing, Training, and Raising a Dog,* New York: Alpha Books, 1996.

Hodgson, Sarah, *DogPerfect*, New York: Howell Book House, 1995.

Trick Training

Baer, Ted, *How to Teach Your Old Dog New Tricks,* Hauppauge, NY: Barron's, 1991.

Benjamin, Carol Lea and Capt. Arthur Haggerty, *Dog Tricks,* New York: Howell Book House, 1987.

Pryor, Karen, *Don't Shoot the Dog!,* New York: Bantam Books, 1984.

Specific Activities

Bauman, Diane, *Beyond Basic Dog Training,* New York: Howell Book House, 1991.

Beaman, Arthur, *Lure Coursing,* New York: Howell Book House, 1994.

Bloeme, Peter, *Frisbee Dogs*, Atlanta: PRB & Associates, 1994.

Davis, Kathy Diamond, *Therapy Dogs, Training Your Dog to Reach Others*, New York: Howell Book House, 1992.

Flanders, Noel K., *The Joy of Running Sled Dogs*, Loveland, Colorado: Alpine Publications, 1989.

Haggerty, Capt. Arthur, *How to Get Your Pet Into Show Business*, New York: Howell Book House, 1994.

Holland, Vergil S., *Herding Dogs, Progressive Training*, New York: Howell Book House, 1994.

Johnson, Glen, *Tracking Dog: Theory and Methods*, Canastota, NY: Arner Publications, 1975.

Koehler, William R., *Training Tracking Dogs*, New York: Howell Book House, 1987.

Medcalf, Bill, *Retrieve*, Southlake, Illinois: Taylor Publishing Company, 1987.

Migliorini, Mario, *Dig In! Earthdog Training Made Easy*, New York: Howell Book House, 1997.

Olsen, Lonnie, *Flyball Racing*, New York: Howell Book House, 1997.

Payne, Joan, *Flying High: The Complete Book of Flyball*, Aurora, CO: KDB Publishing Company, 1996.

Simmons-Moake, Jane, *Agility Training*, New York: Howell Book House, 1991.

Spencer, James B., *Hup! Training Flushing Spaniels the American Way*, New York: Howell Book House, 1992.

Spencer, James B., *Point! Training the All-Seasons Birddog*, New York: Howell Book House, 1995.

Smith, Cheryl S., *On the Trail With Your Canine Companion*, New York: Howell Book House, 1996.

Volhard, Jack and Wendy, *Open and Utility Training: The Motivational Method*, New York: Howell Book House, 1992.

Videos

Hobdy, Ruth, *Control Exercises*, United States Dog Agility Association, 1991.

Hodgson, Sarah, *DogPerfect*, Cooperative Canine Corp., 1996.

Ostrander, Beth, *An Introduction to Canine Carting*.

Owens, Mary, *The ABC's of Dog Training*, Canine University, Pensacola, Florida.

Take a Bow Wow, Take a Bow Wow, 1995.

Index

U-V

W

Z

Tools for Teaching Your Trickster!

 THE TEACHING LEAD®
For going over the basics and for hours of hands-free walking enjoyment! Patented by Ms. Hodgson, this leash is a cool and humane training tool.

 THE TEACHING LEAD® VIDEO
Need a brush-up on the basics? This video's sure to help.

 THE SEAT BELT SAFETY LEAD/ SHORT LEAD
A sure-fire way to calm your canine in the car, and gain quick control around the house.

④ BINACA MOUTH SPRAY®
A tasty way to curb your dog's unmannerly behavior.

⑤ CLICKERS
Sarah Says: Click a Trick. These lively clickers will give your trick training a spin!

ORDER NOW!

**Sarah Hodgson
Cooperative Canine Corp.
P.O. Box 420
Bedford Village, NY 10506**

The Teaching Lead®...$19.95
The Teaching Lead® Video $24.95
The Seat Belt Safety Lead/Short Lead .... $ 9.95
Order all three items for only $49.95

Binaca Mouth Spray®...$ 2.00
Clicker...$2.50 each/pack of five $10.00

Please add:
   Shipping and handling $4.00
   6.75% New York Sales Tax .... $_____

My check for $_____ is enclosed.

Please make your check payable to the Cooperative Canine Corp.

DOG'S NAME AND BREED _____

YOUR NAME _____

YOUR ADDRESS _____

CITY _____ STATE _____ ZIP CODE _____

DAYTIME PHONE _____